EUROPE

Angelika Taschen

GREAT ESCAPES EUROPE

THE HOTEL BOOK

TASCHEN

CONTENTS

KAKSLAUTTANEN
ARCTIC RESORT

SAARISELKÄ, LAPLAND, FINLAND

KAKSLAUTTANEN ARCTIC RESORT

Kiilopääntie 9, 99830 Saariselkä, Finland
Tel. +358 16 667 101 · reservations@kakslauttanen.fi
www.kakslauttanen.fi

IN THE HIGH NORTH

When Jussi Eiramo was returning from the north of Finland back to the middle of the country in 1973 after an angling trip, he ran out of petrol – in the middle of nowhere, at a place called Kakslauttanen, which translates into something like "two stores of reindeer meat". He spent the night in this wilderness and for some reason felt so good there that he pitched his tent for the summer. The following year he came back, built a hut and opened a café for tourists on their way to the North Cape. In the meantime, this one-man business has become Finland's most famous Arctic resort: guests come from every continent, especially in the cold season, to have themselves pulled across a winter wonderland on husky or reindeer sleds, to immerse themselves in icy water at temperatures far below freezing, followed by a sauna – and above all, to see the northern lights flitting across the sky just once in their lives. Thanks to Jussi they don't have to go outside to do this, or even leave their beds: he designed igloos made from thermal glass. Through this transparent cover, the surreal, fantastic colors of the northern lights shine straight into the igloos. But in summer, too, when the sun never seems to set, it is worth taking the trip to Kakslauttanen. Then the best activities are to spend the night in wooden huts made from tree trunks up to 700 years old and explore Finland's fascinating natural world on foot, on a mountain bike or in a canoe. ◆ Book to pack: "Under the North Star" by Väinö Linna.

DIRECTIONS *In Lapland 250 km/155 miles north of the Arctic Circle, 30 minutes' drive from the regional airport at Ivalo (regular flights to Helsinki)* · RATES *€€€–€€€€, incl. breakfast and dinner* · ROOMS *About 170 snow igloos, glass igloos, wood-and-glass igloos, wooden huts, wooden houses, suites, totalling 450 beds* · FOOD *The Lapland restaurants Kelo and Aurora* · HISTORY *The founder Jussi Eiramo still pulls the strings in the background after 45 years* · X-FACTOR *A winter wedding in a snow chapel*

HOCH IM NORDEN

Als Jussi Eiramo 1973 von einem Angelausflug im Norden Finnlands ins Landesinnere zurückfuhr, ging ihm das Benzin aus – mitten im Nirgendwo, an einem Ort namens Kakslauttanen, was übersetzt so viel bedeutet wie „zwei Rentierfleischlager". Er übernachtete in der Wildnis und fühlte sich aus irgendeinem Grund so wohl, dass er sein Zelt den Sommer über aufgeschlagen ließ. Im nächsten Jahr kam er wieder, baute eine Hütte und eröffnete ein Café für Touristen auf ihrem Weg ans Nordkap. Inzwischen ist aus dem Einmannbetrieb Finnlands berühmtestes arktisches Resort geworden: Von allen Kontinenten und vor allem in der kalten Jahreszeit kommen Gäste, um sich auf Husky- oder Rentierschlitten durch ein Winterwunderland ziehen zu lassen, bei Temperaturen weit unter dem Gefrierpunkt ins Eiswasser zu tauchen und anschließend zu saunieren – und vor allem um einmal im Leben Polarlichter über den Himmel huschen zu sehen. Dank Jussi muss man für Letzteres nicht nach draußen und noch nicht einmal aus dem Bett gehen: Er hat Iglus aus Thermoglas entworfen, durch deren transparente Hüllen die surrealen, fantastischen Farben der Polarlichter direkt ins Innere der Behausungen scheinen. Doch auch im Sommer, wenn die Sonne so gut wie nie untergeht, lohnt sich eine Reise nach Kakslauttanen. Dann wohnt man am schönsten in Holzhütten aus bis zu 700 Jahre alten Baumstämmen und entdeckt Finnlands faszinierende Natur beim Wandern, auf dem Mountainbike oder im Kanu. ◆ Buchtipp: „Hier unter dem Polarstern" von Väinö Linna.

ANREISE *In Lappland 250 km nördlich des Polarkreises gelegen, 30 Min. Fahrt mit dem Auto vom regionalen Flughafen Ivalo entfernt (regelmäßige Verbindungen nach Helsinki)* · PREIS *€€€–€€€€, mit Frühstück und Abendessen* · ZIMMER *Rund 170 Unterkünfte mit 450 Betten (Schnee-Iglus, Glas-Iglus, Holz-Glas-Iglus, Holzhütten und -häuser, Suiten)* · KÜCHE *Zwei lappische Restaurants, „Kelo" und „Aurora"* · GESCHICHTE *Gründer Jussi Eiramo zieht auch nach 45 Jahren noch immer die Fäden im Hintergrund* · X-FAKTOR *Die Schneekapelle für Hochzeitspaare*

HAUT DANS LE NORD

Rentrant à l'intérieur des terres en 1973 après un voyage de pêche dans le Nord de la Finlande, Jussi Eiramo est tombé en panne d'essence au milieu de nulle part, dans un endroit appelé Kakslauttanen, ce qui signifie « deux réserves de viande de renne ». Il a passé la nuit dans la nature et, pour une raison ou une autre, s'est senti tellement à l'aise qu'il a dressé ici sa tente pendant tout l'été. Il est revenu l'année suivante, a construit une cabane et ouvert un café pour les touristes en route vers le cap Nord. Aujourd'hui, l'ancienne entreprise unipersonnelle est le complexe touristique arctique le plus célèbre de Finlande : surtout pendant la saison froide, les visiteurs viennent de tous les continents pour traverser un paradis hivernal sur des traîneaux tirés par des huskies ou des rennes, plonger dans l'eau glacée à des températures bien inférieures au point de congélation, puis aller au sauna – et surtout pour voir, une fois dans leur vie, les aurores boréales briller dans le ciel. Grâce à Jussi, vous n'avez pas besoin de sortir ni même de sortir du lit pour les observer ; il a conçu des igloos transparents en verre thermique : les couleurs surréalistes et fantastiques des aurores polaires brillent directement à l'intérieur des habitations. Mais un voyage à Kakslauttanen en vaut la peine même en été, quand le soleil ne se couche presque jamais. On habite alors dans des cabanes en bois faites des troncs d'arbres dont l'âge peut atteindre 700 ans, et on découvre les paysages fascinants de la Finlande en faisant de la randonnée, du VTT ou du canoë. ◆ À lire : « Ici, sous l'étoile polaire » de Väinö Linna.

ACCÈS *En Laponie, à 250 km au nord du cercle polaire, à 30 min de voiture de l'aéroport régional d'Ivalo (liaisons régulières avec Helsinki)* · PRIX *€€€–€€€€, petit déjeuner et dîner inclus* · CHAMBRES *Environ 170 hébergements avec 450 lits (igloos classiques, igloos de verre, igloos en bois, cabanes et maison en bois, suites)* · RESTAURATION *Deux restaurants «Kelo» et «Aurora», spécialités laponnes* · HISTOIRE *Le fondateur Jussi Eiramo continue, 45 ans plus tard, de tirer les ficelles en coulisses* · LES « PLUS » *La chapelle de glace où l'on peut se marier*

BUDSJORD PILGRIMSGÅRDEN

DOVRE, NORWAY

BUDSJORD
PILGRIMSGÅRDEN

Øverbygdsvegen 145, 2662 Dovre, Norway
Tel: + 47 982 863 98 and + 47 916 062 37 · post@budsjord.no
www.budsjord.no
Open from 21 June, the longest day of the year, to mid-August

TRAVEL FOR ITS OWN SAKE

This is one of the loneliest pilgrimage routes in the world: along St Olaf's Way from Oslo to Trondheim you encounter more sheep, musk oxen and reindeer than people. Long ago the Viking King Olaf II (Haraldsson; 955–1030) passed this way to convert the heathen Norwegians to Christianity. Now the route is a destination for travellers who want to walk through one of the most spectacular landscapes in Scandinavia. The last stop before Dovrefjell National Park with its rocky plateaus, moors and lakes is Budsjord. Originally owned by the church, this estate provided accommodation for the bishop on pilgrimage, then passed to the king for a short time, and finally came into the hands of private families who were excellent wood carvers, smiths and engravers: many paintings and pieces of furniture inside the houses are originals dating from the 18th and 19th centuries. The owners, an art historian and an architect with ancestors from this area, restored the estate, which is a designated monument, with the help of local craftworkers and a sensitivity to tradition. They retained the idea of dormitories, a bathhouse and a communal table, but modernised the 18 grass-roofed wooden houses, and plan to add a museum and a library in the years to come. ◆ Book to pack: "An Unreliable Man" by Jostein Gaarder.

DIRECTIONS *290 km/180 miles from Oslo airport, 240 km from Trondheim airport* · **RATES** *€ (dormitory) – €€ (double room), both including breakfast, a packed lunch and a simple evening meal* · **ROOMS** *10 rooms with a total of 25 beds* · **FOOD** *Dovre is surrounded by fertile land. A local cook prepares traditional dishes from regional products according to old recipes* · **HISTORY** *The oldest written sources about the estate date from the 15th century. Since 2012 it belongs to E. Fenstad Langdalen and V. Plahte Tschudi* · **X-FACTOR** *The estate has been awarded an Olavsrosa for Norwegian cultural heritage*

DER WEG IST DAS ZIEL

Er ist einer der einsamsten Pilgerwege der Welt: Entlang des Olavswegs zwischen Oslo und Trondheim trifft man mehr Schafe, Moschusochsen und Rentiere als Menschen. Einst zog der Wikingerkönig Olav II. Haraldsson (955–1030) hier entlang, um den heidnischen Norwegern das Christentum zu bringen – jetzt ist der Weg das Ziel von Reisenden, die ganz in Ruhe eine der spektakulärsten Landschaften Skandinaviens erwandern wollen. Letzte Station vor dem Nationalpark Dovrefjell mit seinen Felsplateaus, Mooren und Seen ist der Budsjord. Ursprünglich im Besitz der Kirche bot der Hof dem pilgernden Bischof Unterkunft, ging dann kurz an den König über und schließlich an Privatfamilien, die hervorragende Holzschnitzer, Schmiede sowie Graveure waren: Zahlreiche Malereien und Möbel im Inneren der Häuser sind Originale aus dem 18. und 19. Jahrhundert. Die heutigen Besitzer, ein Kunsthistoriker und ein Architekt mit Vorfahren aus der Gegend, restaurierten den denkmalgeschützten Hof mithilfe einheimischer Handwerker und viel Gespür für Traditionen. Sie behielten die Idee von Schlaflagern, einem Badehaus sowie einer Gemeinschaftstafel bei – modernisierten und erweiterten die 18 grasgedeckten Holzhäuser jedoch und planen, in den kommenden Jahren ein Bauernmuseum und eine Bibliothek hinzuzufügen. ◆ Buchtipp: „Ein treuer Freund" von Jostein Gaarder.

ANREISE *290 km vom Flughafen Oslo, 240 km vom Flughafen Trondheim entfernt* · PREIS *€ (Schlaflager) – €€ (Doppelzimmer), jeweils mit Frühstück, Stullenpaket und einfachem Abendessen* · ZIMMER *10 Zimmer mit insgesamt 25 Betten* · KÜCHE *Rund um Dovre liegt fruchtbares Land – aus lokalen Produkten und nach alten Rezepten bereitet eine einheimische Köchin traditionelle Speisen zu* · GESCHICHTE *Die ältesten Quellen über den Hof stammen aus dem 15. Jahrhundert. Seit 2012 gehört das Anwesen E. Fenstad Langdalen und V. Plahte Tschudi* · X-FAKTOR *Der Hof ist mit der „Olavsrosa" als norwegisches Kulturerbe ausgezeichnet*

LE CHEMIN EST LE BUT

Le chemin de Saint-Olaf, entre Oslo et Trondheim, est l'un des chemins de pèlerinage les plus solitaires qui soient, et vous y rencontrerez plus de moutons, de bœufs musqués et de rennes que d'êtres humains. Le roi viking Olav II Haraldsson (955–1030) l'a emprunté autrefois pour propager la foi chrétienne parmi les Norvégiens païens – aujourd'hui le sentier est foulé par des voyageurs qui veulent explorer l'un des paysages les plus spectaculaires de Scandinavie en toute tranquillité. Le dernier arrêt avant le parc national de Dovrefjell avec ses plateaux rocheux, ses landes et ses lacs est le Budsjord. Propriété de l'Église à l'origine, la ferme a hébergé l'évêque pèlerin, avant de passer brièvement au roi et enfin à des familles privées dont les membres étaient de remarquables sculpteurs sur bois, forgerons et graveurs : de nombreuses peintures et meubles à l'intérieur des maisons sont des originaux des XVIIIe et XIXe siècles. Les propriétaires actuels, un historien de l'art et un architecte dont les ancêtres vivaient dans la région, ont restauré la ferme classée avec l'aide d'artisans locaux et un sens aigu des traditions. Ils ont conservé l'idée de dortoirs, de maison de bains et de grand table commune, mais ils ont modernisé et agrandi les 18 maisons en bois et ont prévu d'ajouter un musée agricole et une bibliothèque dans les années à venir. ◆ À lire : « Dukkeføreren » de Jostein Gaarder.

ACCÈS *À 290 km de l'aéroport d'Oslo et à 240 km de l'aéroport de Trondheim* · PRIX *€ (nuit au dortoir) – €€ (chambre double), petit déjeuner, paquet de sandwichs et dîner simple inclus* · CHAMBRES *10 chambres avec 25 lits en tout* · RESTAURATION *La terre est fertile autour de Dovre – une cuisinière de la région prépare des plats traditionnels basés sur des produits locaux et des recettes anciennes* · HISTOIRE *Les sources les plus lointaines remontent au XVe siècle. Depuis 2012, le domaine appartient à E. Fenstad Langdalen et V. Plahte Tschudi* · LES « PLUS » *Distinguée par la « Olavsrosa », la ferme est classée au patrimoine norvégien*

WALAKER HOTELL

SOLVORN, NORWAY

WALAKER HOTELL

6879 Solvorn, Sogn, Norway
Tel: + 47 57 68 20 80 · hotel@walaker.com
www.walaker.com
Open from early April to late October

NORWEGIAN NOSTALGIA

The water sparkles in shades of emerald and turquoise, flowing past rolling hills, steep glacier walls and villages of colorful wooden houses, and the crystal-clear air makes the skin tingle. The extensive fjord region around Bergen is one of the loveliest areas of Norway – and one of the most historic. Here the country's oldest stave church and its oldest inn are to be found. The Hotell Walaker has existed since 1640, and has belonged to the Nitter family almost as long. Ole Henrik Nitter represents the ninth generation to run it (and the tenth generation has already been born). An elevated view of the Sognefjord and a garden with gnarled fruit trees are features of the estate, which has rooms in various buildings. In the main house and Tingstova house are historic rooms with traditional wallpaper, antique furnishings and free-standing painted bathtubs. The bungalow-like annex, which only dates from the mid-20th century, is not quite as stylish, but to compensate the rooms here have their own veranda. Daytime activities include a stroll through the likeable little town of Solvorn, a trip by ferry to nearby harbors, or a hike through the national park of Jostedalsbreen, the biggest glacier in continental Europe. But guests should be back at the Hotell Walaker in good time, as a Norwegian four-course menu is served at 7.30 pm on the dot. ◆ Book to pack: "Bergeners" by Tomas Espedal.

DIRECTIONS *Solvorn lies 230 km/140 miles north-east of Bergen, 35 km/22 miles from the regional airport at Sogndal* · **RATES** *€€€ (room in annex) – €€€€ (room in main house and Tsingtova)* · **ROOMS** *25 rooms* · **FOOD** *All ingredients for the restaurant are supplied from the surrounding region* · **HISTORY** *The hotel was originally a trading post. The Nitter family bought it in 1690* · **X-FACTOR** *The in-house art gallery*

NORWEGISCHE NOSTALGIE

Das Wasser schimmert in Smaragd- und Türkistönen, fließt an sanften Hügeln, steilen Gletscherwänden und Dörfern mit bunten Holzhäusern vorbei, und die kristallklare Luft prickelt: Die weite Fjordregion rund um Bergen ist eine der schönsten Gegenden Norwegens – und eine der geschichtsträchtigsten: Hier steht nicht nur die älteste Stabkirche des Landes, sondern auch das älteste Gasthaus. Seit 1640 gibt es das Hotell Walaker, und fast genauso lange gehört es der Familie Nitter. Ole Henrik Nitter führt es in neunter Generation (und auch die zehnte Generation ist schon geboren). Ein Logenblick auf den Sognefjord sowie ein Garten mit knorrigen Obstbäumen gehören ebenso zum Anwesen wie verschiedene Gebäude mit Gästezimmern. Im Haupthaus und der „Tingstova" befinden sich die historischen Räume mit traditionellen Tapeten, antiken Möbeln und frei stehenden bemalten Badewannen. Nicht ganz so stilvoll präsentiert sich der bungalowartige Anbau, der erst Mitte des 20. Jahrhunderts entstand, doch dafür haben die Zimmer eine eigene Veranda. Tagsüber kann man durch das sympathische Städtchen Solvorn spazieren, mit der Fähre die nahen Häfen ansteuern oder durch den Nationalpark am Jostedalsbreen wandern, dem größten Gletscher auf europäischem Festland. Pünktlich um 19.30 Uhr sollten Hotelgäste aber wieder im Walaker sein, denn auf die Minute genau wird ein norwegisches Vier-Gänge-Menü serviert. ◆ Buchtipp: „Bergeners" von Tomas Espedal.

ANREISE *Solvorn liegt 230 km nordöstlich von Bergen, 35 km vom regionalen Flughafen Sogndal entfernt ·* **PREIS** *€€€ (Zimmer im Anbau) – €€€€ (Zimmer in Haupthaus und Tingstova) ·* **ZIMMER** *25 Zimmer ·* **KÜCHE** *Das Restaurant bezieht alle Zutaten aus der Region ·* **GESCHICHTE** *Ursprünglich war das Hotel ein Handelsposten. Die Familie Nitter kaufte es 1690 ·* **X-FAKTOR** *Die hauseigene Kunstgalerie*

NOSTALGIE NORVÉGIENNE

Une eau scintillante aux tons d'émeraude et de turquoise coule le long de douces collines, de parois de glace abruptes et de villages aux maisons de bois colorées, et l'air est limpide : le vaste fjord autour de Bergen est l'une des plus belles régions de Norvège – et l'une des plus intéressantes sur le plan historique, puisqu'on y trouve la plus vieille église en bois et la plus ancienne auberge du pays. L'hôtel Walaker existe depuis 1640 et appartient à la famille Nitter depuis presque aussi longtemps. Il est aujourd'hui dirigé par la neuvième génération avec Ole Henrik Nitter (et la dixième génération est déjà née). La vue sur le Sognefjord et un jardin où poussent des arbres fruitiers noueux font partie de la propriété ainsi que divers bâtiments avec chambres. La maison principale et la « Tingstova » abritent des pièces historiques avec leur papier peint traditionnel, des meubles anciens et des baignoires sur pied peintes. L'extension en forme de bungalow, qui n'a été construite qu'au milieu du XXe siècle, n'est pas aussi élégante, mais ses chambres ont leur propre véranda. Pendant la journée, vous pouvez vous promener dans la plaisante petite ville de Solvorn, prendre un ferry pour vous rendre dans les ports voisins ou faire une randonnée dans le parc national de Jostedalsbreen, le plus grand glacier d'Europe continentale. Mais il vous faudra être de retour au Walaker à l'heure, car un repas norvégien à quatre plats est servi à 19 h 30 pile. ◆ À lire : « Gens de Bergen » de Tomas Espedal.

ACCÈS *Solvorn est située à 230 km au nord-est de Bergen, à 35 km de l'aéroport régional de Sogndal ·* **PRIX** *€€€ (chambre dans l'annexe) – €€€€ (chambre dans la maison principale et Tingstova) ·* **CHAMBRES** *25 chambres ·* **RESTAURATION** *Le restaurant s'approvisionne directement en produits frais dans les alentours ·* **HISTOIRE** *À l'origine, l'hôtel était un comptoir de commerce. La famille Nitter l'a acheté en 1690 ·* **LES « PLUS »** *L'hôtel a sa propre galerie d'art*

HELENEKILDE
BADEHOTEL

TISVILDELEJE, ON THE KATTEGAT, DENMARK

HELENEKILDE BADEHOTEL

3220 Tisvildeleje, Denmark
Tel: + 45 48 70 70 01 · kontakt@helenekilde.com
www.helenekilde.com

THE BEACH HOUSE

Some people refer to the stretch of coast north of Copenhagen as the Danish Riviera or Ile de Ré, while others call it the Scandinavian Hamptons – high-class comparisons, although none of them is one hundred per cent accurate because, here, Denmark is just Denmark, so simple, beautiful and natural, so full of sun and sand, woods and water, dunes and design that all the hygge and Scandi-chic magazines could effortlessly fill a year's worth of issues. The most photogenic address in pretty Tisvildeleje is, without a doubt, the hotel Helenekilde. Originally built by a Copenhagen real-estate baron as a summer residence for his wife, it was converted to a hotel in the early twentieth century and now belongs to the Kølpin family, whose members are among the most creative people in the country. Alexander Kølpin, once an award-winning dancer at the Royal Danish Ballet and now a globe-trotting choreographer and director, was responsible for the design at Helenekilde: the rooms, in beach-house style throughout the house, reflect the shades of white and blue of the surroundings, are furnished with lots of wood and rattan, and decorated with pictures, books and flowers. The atmosphere is relaxed, straightforward, almost with a family touch – here luxury is a feeling, not ostentation. In summer guests spend their wonderfully long vacation days swimming and sunbathing – the beach is right on the doorstep – and the mild winters are a time for exploring the coast on walks or by bike. The perfect way to round off each day is the Nordic evening menu in the hotel – and a sundowner with a sea view that stretches to the horizon.
♦ Book to pack: "The Susan Effect" by Peter Høeg.

DIRECTIONS *55 km/35 miles north of Copenhagen; near Helene Kilde, Denmark's best-known healing spring, which gave the hotel its name ·* RATES *€€–€€€ ·* ROOMS *28 rooms and suites. Don't fail to book one with a sea view ·* FOOD *Modern Danish cuisine: breakfast, lunch à la carte and a set three-course evening meal ·* HISTORY *Built in 1896, a hotel since 1904. Alexander Kølpin renovated the house in 2008 ·* X-FACTOR *On request, yoga sessions and massage in the garden pavilion can be arranged*

DAS STRANDHAUS

Manche nennen diesen Küstenabschnitt nördlich von Kopenhagen die dänische Riviera oder Ile de Ré, andere sprechen von den Hamptons Skandinaviens – hochrangige Vergleiche, von denen es jedoch keiner hundertprozentig trifft. Denn hier ist Dänemark einfach Dänemark: so schlicht, schön und natürlich, so voller Sonne und Sand, Wald und Wasser, Dünen und Design, dass sämtliche Hygge- und Skandischick-Magazine mühelos ganze Jahrgänge füllen könnten. Fotogenste Adresse im hübschen Ort Tisvildeleje ist ohne Frage das Helenekilde. Ursprünglich von einem Kopenhagener Immobilienmagnaten als Sommersitz für seine Frau erbaut, wurde es Anfang des 20. Jahrhunderts in ein Hotel verwandelt und gehört heute der Familie Kølpin, deren Mitglieder zu den kreativsten Köpfen des Landes zählen. Alexander Kølpin, früher preisgekrönter Tänzer beim Königlich Dänischen Ballett und als Choreograph sowie Regisseur in aller Welt unterwegs, entwarf das Design des Helenekilde: Ganz im Strandhaus-Stil gehalten, spiegeln die Räume die Weiß- und Blautöne der Umgebung wider, sind mit viel Holz und Rattan ausgestattet und mit Bildern, Büchern sowie Blumen verschönt. Die Atmosphäre ist entspannt, unkompliziert, fast familiär – Luxus ist hier ein Gefühl, keine Demonstration. Im Sommer verbringt man die wunderbar langen Ferientage mit Schwimmen und Sonnenbaden (der Strand liegt direkt vor der Tür), im milden Winter lässt sich die Küste bei Spaziergängen oder Radtouren erkunden. Perfekter Abschluss eines jeden Tages ist das nordische Abendmenü im Hotel – und der Schlummertrunk mit Blick über die See bis zum Horizont. ◆ Buchtipp: „Der Susan-Effekt" von Peter Høeg.

ANREISE *55 km nördlich von Kopenhagen gelegen; nahe der „Helene Kilde", Dänemarks berühmtester Heilquelle, die dem Hotel seinen Namen gab* · PREIS *€€–€€€* · ZIMMER *28 Zimmer und Suiten. Unbedingt Meerblick buchen!* · KÜCHE *Moderne dänische Küche: Frühstück, Lunch à la carte und festes 3-Gänge-Menü am Abend* · GESCHICHTE *1896 erbaut und seit 1904 ein Hotel. Alexander Kølpin renovierte das Haus 2008* · X-FAKTOR *Auf Wunsch werden Yogastunden und Massagen im Gartenpavillon angeboten*

LA MAISON DE PLAGE

Cette partie de la côte, au nord de Copenhague, est parfois nommée la Riviera danoise ou l'île de Ré, on parle aussi des Hamptons scandinaves – des comparaisons flatteuses, bien qu'aucune ne corresponde parfaitement à la réalité. Parce qu'ici, le Danemark est tout simplement le Danemark : si simple, si beau et naturel, si plein de soleil et de sable, de forêt et d'eau, de dunes et de design que les journalistes pourraient facilement remplir tous les magazines Hygge et Skandischick pendant des années. L'hôtel Helenekilde est sans aucun doute l'adresse la plus photogénique de la jolie ville de Tisvildeleje. Construit à l'origine par un magnat copenhaguois de l'immobilier comme résidence d'été pour son épouse, il a été transformé en hôtel au début du XXe siècle et appartient aujourd'hui à la famille Kølpin, qui compte parmi ses membres les personnes les plus créatives du pays. Alexander Kølpin, ancien danseur primé du Ballet royal danois et qui a travaillé comme chorégraphe et metteur en scène dans le monde entier, a conçu l'Helenekilde dans un style de maison de plage : les pièces qui reflètent les tons de blanc et de bleu du paysage environnant sont meublées de bois et de rotin et décorées de tableaux, de livres et de fleurs. Tout est facile, l'atmosphère est détendue, presque familière – ici le luxe ne s'expose pas, les hôtes le ressentent. En été, vous passez de merveilleuses vacances à nager et à prendre des bains de soleil (la plage est au pied de la porte) ; l'hiver étant doux, vous pouvez explorer la côte à pied ou en bicyclette. Et pour terminer la journée, rien de tel que le dîner nordique à l'hôtel et le digestif avec vue sur la mer jusqu'à l'horizon. ◆ À lire : « Le pouvoir de Susan » de Peter Høeg.

ACCÈS *Situé à 55 km au nord de Copenhague ; à proximité de la « Helene Kilde », la source d'eau minérale la plus célèbre du Danemark, qui a donné son nom à l'établissement* · PRIX *€€–€€€* · CHAMBRES *28 chambres et suites. La vue sur la mer est un must !* · RESTAURATION *Cuisine danoise moderne: petit déjeuner, déjeuner à la carte et menu à trois plats le soir* · HISTOIRE *Construit en 1896 et utilisé comme hôtel depuis 1904. Alexander Kølpin a rénové la maison en 2008* · LES « PLUS » *Des cours de yoga et des massages dans le pavillon de jardin sont proposés sur demande*

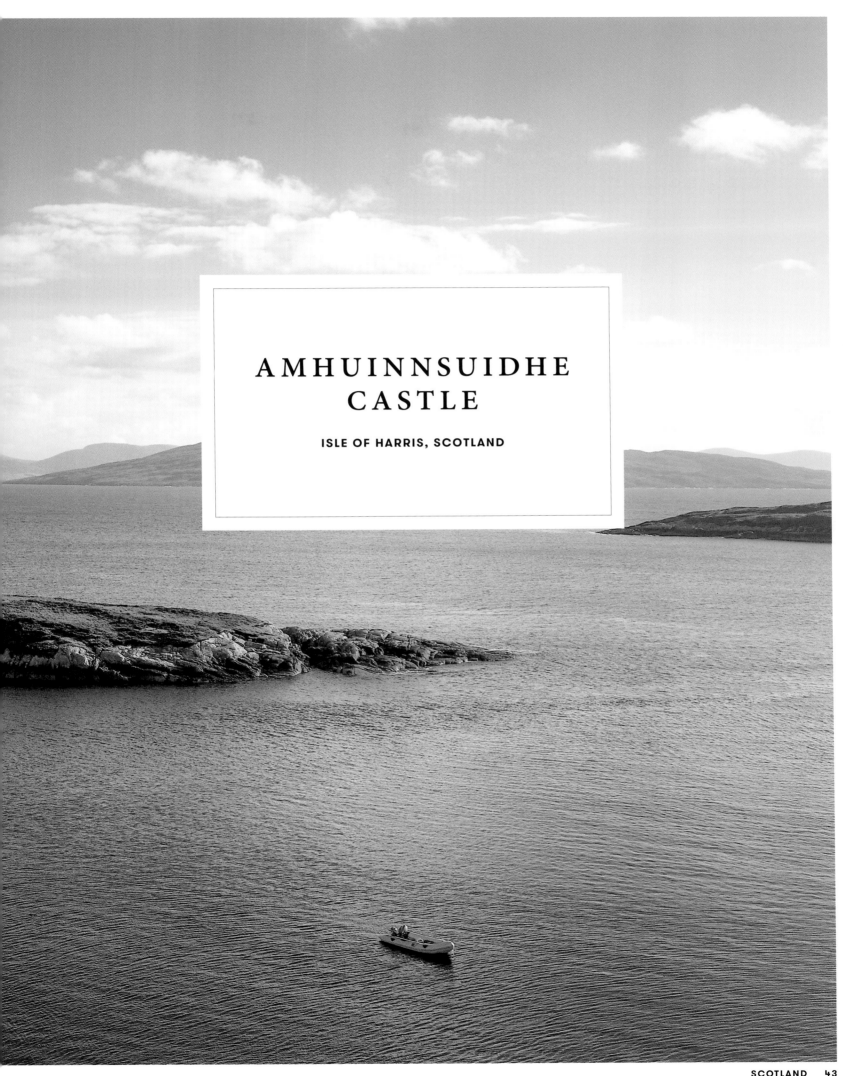

AMHUINNSUIDHE CASTLE

ISLE OF HARRIS, SCOTLAND

AMHUINNSUIDHE CASTLE

Isle of Harris, Hebrides PA85 3AS, Scotland
Tel: + 44 1876 500 329 · info@amhuinnsuidhe.com
www.amhuinnsuidhe.com

A CASTLE OF ONE'S OWN

A man's home is his castle, or so goes that old saw. Would that you could make this castle your home, at least for a time, quite set apart from the rest of the world. Amhuinnsuidhe Castle, on the Isle of Harris, is the most westerly castle in the whole United Kingdom. Built more than one hundred years ago, it stands at the edge of the sea in dramatic and beautiful surroundings. The castle's domain covers many thousands of acres, and is one of Europe's last unspoilt wildernesses. Although it is privately owned, it can be yours for a week. Set in a rugged landscape of mountains and glens, lochs and rivers, and white sandy beaches, it is world famous for its salmon and sea trout fishing. And it was here that the weaving of the classic Harris Tweed fabric first began. This castle on the beach, sheltered at the head of its own bay, is known for its good food: the team liberally uses the ingredients that nature makes available so plentifully here. Rosemary, the castle's chef and host of a television cookery programme, makes full use of the rich local resources – lobsters and scallops fresh from the sea as well as venison and lamb. ◆ Books to pack: "Mary Stuart" by Friedrich Schiller and "Ivanhoe" by Sir Walter Scott.

DIRECTIONS *There is anchorage in front of the castle and a helicopter landing site. Stornoway airport on the Isle of Harris, 1 hour by road, is 40 minutes flying time from Inverness, 1 hour from Glasgow ·* RATES *€€ ·* ROOMS *12 individually designed rooms ·* FOOD *Fresh fish and shellfish ·* HISTORY *Built for the Earl of Dunmore in 1867 ·* X-FACTOR *Romantic isolation and picturesque landscape*

EIN SCHLOSS FÜR SICH ALLEIN

„My home is my castle" lautet ein altes englisches Sprichwort. Dieser Traum vom eigenen Schloss kann Wirklichkeit werden an einem Ort weit entfernt vom Rest der Welt. Das auf der malerischen Isle of Harris gelegene Amhuinnsuidhe Castle ist die am westlichsten gelegene Burg Großbritanniens. Sie wurde vor mehr als hundert Jahren direkt an der Küste inmitten einer aufregenden Landschaft erbaut. Über mehrere Tausend Hektar erstrecken sich die angrenzenden Ländereien, welche zu den letzten Flecken unberührter Natur in Europa gehören. Obwohl sich die Burg in Privatbesitz befindet, ist es möglich, sie für eine Woche sein Eigen zu nennen. Umgeben von zerklüfteten Bergen und Tälern, Seen und Flüssen sowie weißen Sandstränden, ist sie weltberühmt für den Fang von Lachs und Meeresforellen. Und hier war es auch, wo man anfing, den klassischen Harris Tweed zu weben. Diese am Strand, im Schutz ihrer eigenen Bucht gelegene Burg ist auch für gute Küche bekannt: Das Team macht großzügigen Gebrauch von dem, was die Natur hier in reichlichem Maße bietet: Hummer und Kammmuscheln frisch aus dem Meer sowie Wild und Lamm. ◆ Buchtipps: „Maria Stuart" von Friedrich Schiller und „Ivanhoe" von Sir Walter Scott.

ANREISE *Die Burg verfügt über eigene Ankerplätze und einen Hubschrauberlandeplatz. Von Inverness zum Flughafen Stornoway auf der Isle of Harris 40 Min., von Glasgow 1 Std. Flugzeit, vom Flughafen Stornoway 1 Std. Fahrt ·* **PREIS** *€€ ·* **ZIMMER** *12 individuell gestaltete Zimmer ·* **KÜCHE** *Frischer Fisch und Muscheln ·* **GESCHICHTE** *Im Jahr 1867 für den Earl of Dunmore erbaut ·* **X-FAKTOR** *Romantische Einsamkeit und malerische Landschaft*

UN CHÂTEAU POUR SOI

« Mon chez-moi est mon château », dit un proverbe britannique. Qui n'a pas rêvé parfois de posséder sa propre forteresse et de vivre dans un château, loin du reste du monde… Amhuinnsuidhe Castle, sur l'île de Harris, est le château situé le plus à l'ouest de la Grande-Bretagne. Construit il y a plus d'un siècle, il se dresse au bord de la mer, à l'abri d'une baie privative, dans un environnement de toute beauté. Le domaine, qui couvre quelques milliers d'hectares, est l'un des derniers sanctuaires sauvages d'Europe. Bien que privée, cette demeure seigneuriale peut être la vôtre pendant une semaine. Nichée dans un rude paysage de montagnes, de glens, de lochs, de rivières et de plages de sable blanc, elle jouit d'une renommée internationale pour la pêche au saumon et à la truite de mer. C'est également ici que naquirent les célèbres filatures Harris Tweed. Ce château en bord de mer, situé à l'abri de sa baie, est également connu pour sa bonne cuisine : l'équipe utilise généreusement ce que la nature offre ici en abondance : les homards, les coquilles Saint-Jacques, l'agneau et le gibier. ◆ À lire : « Marie Stuart » de Friedrich Schiller et « Ivanhoé » de Sir Walter Scott.

ACCÈS *Il existe un mouillage devant le château et un héliport. L'aéroport de Stornoway sur l'île de Harris est à 1 h de route; il relie Inverness en 40 min et Glasgow en 1 h ·* **PRIX** *€€ ·* **CHAMBRES** *12 chambres de style individuel ·* **RESTAURATION** *Poisson frais, moules ·* **HISTOIRE** *Construit en 1867 pour le duc de Dunmore ·* **LES « PLUS »** *Isolement romantique et paysage grandiose*

KILLIEHUNTLY
FARMHOUSE

KINGUSSIE, HIGHLANDS, SCOTLAND

KILLIEHUNTLY FARMHOUSE

By Kingussie, Highland PH21 1NZ, Scotland
Tel. + 44 1540 661 619 · hello@killiehuntly.scot
www.killiehuntly.scot
Open from March to December

DENMARK IN SCOTLAND

What do you get when you cross contemporary Danish design with the atmosphere of a traditional Scottish country house? "Scandi-Scot" – this is how Anders Holch Povlsen and Anne Storm Pedersen describe the unique style of Killiehuntly, their hideaway in the Highlands. Anders, a Danish fashion magnate and billionaire, has loved Scotland since he was a child, and now owns more land there than the British Crown. "Scotland is somewhat masculine. It's about hunting and whisky", says Anne – and counteracts the rather masculine exterior with a more feminine interior: Killiehuntly is decorated in high-class shades of cream, gray and blue, combines the rustic antiques of the previous owner with modern design classics from Denmark, and has rooms adorned with contemporary photographs by Trine Søndergaard as well as Scottish sheep's fleeces and handwoven carpets. In the rooms of the main house, the apartment in the annex and the cottages – everywhere guests enjoy subtle luxury and at the same time surroundings that are so relaxed it feels like you're staying with friends. To match this, breakfast, afternoon tea and dinner are served at two long tables – home-made, seasonal treats using ingredients that come from Killiehuntly's own organic farm. Visitors are spoiled with good food even on trips into the Highlands: for the "pony picnic", horses carry the equipment and walkers' provisions, trotting off to the finest spots for a break. ◆ Book to pack: "Collected Poems" by Robert Burns.

DIRECTIONS *In the Cairngorms National Park, 186 km/115 miles north of Edinburgh airport ·* **RATES** *€€€, rooms with breakfast and dinner, cottages for self-catering ·* **ROOMS** *4 double rooms in the main house (some with their own bathrooms), 1 cottage for 5 guests (minimum stay 3 nights), 1 cottage for 4 guests (minimum stay 3 nights), 1 apartment in the annex for 2 guests ·* **FOOD** *Scottish rustic cooking. The cottages, house and apartment have kitchenettes ·* **HISTORY** *The estate dates from the 1850s ·* **X-FACTOR** *Wonderful design in wonderful natural surroundings*

DÄNEMARK IN SCHOTTLAND

Was kommt heraus, wenn man zeitgenössisches dänisches Design mit traditionellem schottischem Landhausflair kombiniert? „Scandi-Scot" – so bezeichnen zumindest Anders Holch Povlsen und Anne Storm Pedersen den einzigartigen Stil von Killiehuntly, ihres Hideaways in den Highlands. Anders, dänischer Modemagnat und Milliardär, liebt Schottland seit seiner Kindheit und besitzt dort inzwischen mehr Land als das britische Königshaus. „Schottland ist etwas maskulin, es ist Jagd und Whisky", sagt Anne – und setzt dem herben, eher maskulinen Exterieur ein feineres, feminineres Interieur entgegen: Killiehuntly wird in edlen Crème-, Grau- und Blautönen gehalten, kombiniert rustikale Antiquitäten der ehemaligen Besitzerin mit modernen Designklassikern aus Dänemark und schmückt die Räume mit aktuellen Fotografien von Trine Søndergaard ebenso wie mit schottischen Schafsfellen und handgeknüpften Teppichen. Ob in den Zimmern im Haupthaus, dem Apartment im Anbau oder in den Cottages – überall genießt man viel Stil, subtilen Luxus und zugleich ein so unkompliziertes Ambiente, als wäre man zu Gast bei Freunden. Passend dazu werden Frühstück, Afternoon Tea und Abendessen an zwei langen Tafeln serviert – hausgemachte, saisonale Köstlichkeiten aus Zutaten vom eigenen Biohof. Sogar bei Ausflügen in die Highlands werden Besucher kulinarisch verwöhnt: Beim „Pony-Picknick" tragen Pferde Ausrüstung und Verpflegung der Wanderer und traben die schönsten Pausenplätze an. ◆ Buchtipp: „Liebe und Freiheit" von Robert Burns.

ANREISE *Im Cairngorms-Nationalpark gelegen, 186 km nördlich des Flughafens Edinburgh ·* PREIS *€€€, Zimmer mit Frühstück und Abendessen, Cottages mit Selbstverpflegung ·* ZIMMER *4 Doppelzimmer im Haupthaus (teils mit eigenem Bad), 1 Cottage für 5 Gäste (3 Nächte Mindestaufenthalt), 1 Cottage für 4 Gäste (3 Nächte Mindestaufenthalt), 1 Apartment im Anbau für 2 Gäste ·* KÜCHE *Frische, schottische Bauernküche. Cottages und Apartment besitzen auch Kitchenettes ·* GESCHICHTE *Das Anwesen stammt aus den 1850er-Jahren ·* X-FAKTOR *Wunderbares Design inmitten einer wunderbaren Natur*

LE DANEMARK EN ÉCOSSE

Que se passe-t-il si vous mariez le design danois contemporain à l'atmosphère traditionnelle des maisons de campagne écossaises ? « Scandi-Scot », c'est ainsi en tout cas qu'Anders Holch Povlsen et Anne Storm Pedersen qualifient le style unique de Killiehuntly, leur retraite dans les Highlands. Anders, magnat de la mode danoise et milliardaire, est amoureux de l'Écosse depuis son enfance et possède maintenant plus de terres que la famille royale britannique. « L'Écosse est un peu virile, c'est la chasse et le whisky », dit Anne – et oppose à l'extérieur austère et plutôt masculin un intérieur plus raffiné et plus féminin : Killiehuntly est aménagé dans des tons nobles crème, gris et bleu, associe des antiquités rustiques ayant appartenu à l'ancienne propriétaire à des classiques danois du design moderne ; les pièces sont agrémentées de photographies actuelles de Trine Søndergaard, ainsi que de peaux de mouton écossaises et de tapis tissés à la main. Que ce soit dans les pièces du bâtiment principal, dans l'appartement de l'annexe ou dans les cottages – partout on apprécie l'élégance, le luxe subtil et en même temps une ambiance bon enfant, on se croirait invité chez des amis. Le petit déjeuner, le thé de cinq heures et le dîner sont servis à deux longues tables – des délices de saison préparés ici à partir de produits issus de la ferme biologique des propriétaires. Les visiteurs sont choyés même lors des excursions dans les Highlands : des poneys transportent le matériel et la nourriture destinés aux randonneurs et s'arrêtent dans les plus beaux endroits pour pique-niquer. ◆ À lire : « Poésies complètes » de Robert Burns.

ACCÈS *Dans le parc national de Cairngorms, à 186 km au nord de l'aéroport d'Édimbourg ·* PRIX *€€€, chambre double avec petit déjeuner et dîner, cottages sans repas ·* CHAMBRES *4 chambres à coucher dans le bâtiment principal (elles n'ont pas toutes de salles de bains), 1 cottage pour 5 personnes (3 nuits minimum), 1 cottage pour 4 personnes (3 nuits minimum), 1 appartement dans l'annexe pour 2 personnes ·* RESTAURATION *Cuisine écossaise rustique à base de produits frais. Les cottages et l'appartement ont aussi une petite cuisine ·* HISTOIRE *Le domaine date des années 1850 ·* LES « PLUS » *Un design magnifique au milieu d'une nature splendide*

THE GUNTON ARMS

THORPE MARKET, NORWICH, ENGLAND

THE GUNTON ARMS

Cromer Rd, Thorpe Market, Norwich, Norfolk NR11 8TZ, England
Tel: + 44 1263 83 20 10 · office@theguntonarms.co.uk
www.theguntonarms.co.uk

LAND ART LIVING

With the Gunton Arms, art dealer Ivor Braka has set the bar even higher: in 2009, together with his colleague Kit Martin, he bought up the ruins of an old guest house and carried out a detailed renovation programme. With only eight guest rooms, this boutique hotel now operates as a traditional pub. It speaks of British understatement, perhaps even British humor, because although the meat dishes in the Gunton Arms are cooked over an open fire, this technique now betokens real luxury – especially when your chef is Stuart Tattersall, previously responsible for the seafood at Mark Hix's in London's Mayfair. However, the most luxurious feature at the Gunton Arms is outside the front door: this boutique pub lies in the midst of a nature reserve of 400 hectares, where not only foxes and hares, but also owls and deer present their evening greetings from mist-enshrouded meadows. And there are 800 deer, by the way. All of this can be observed from the rooms with their traditional décor and every home comfort – from a velvet-upholstered armchair if you so desire. Or you can heave a sigh, put on your rubber boots and trudge through the dewy meadows as twilight falls. Not only wildlife and nature can be found in the floodplain of the parkland, but also sculptures by Sol LeWitt, Anthony Caro and Dan Graham (among others…). In the dining rooms of the Gunton Arms, also popular among residents of the picturesque environs, hang works by Damien Hirst and Tracey Emin. On a wall in the men's room there is even a work by Araki. Consummate understatement is still welcome in Great Britain: in 2013, the Gunton Arms was selected as Michelin Pub of the Year. ◆ Book to pack: "Jane Eyre" by Charlotte Brontë.

DIRECTIONS *255 km/160 miles north of London Heathrow, 25 minutes from Norwich airport ·* RATES *€€ ·* ROOMS *8 rooms, two living rooms (stamp rooms), which are intended only for hotel guests ·* FOOD *Regional and seasonal ·* HISTORY *The former gatehouse to a park that was created in the 18th century, and opened in 2011 for hotel and pub guests ·* X-FACTOR *English country life surrounded by contemporary art*

STILVOLLES LANDLEBEN

Mit dem Gunton Arms legt der Kunsthändler Ivor Braka die Latte besonders hoch: Gemeinsam mit seinem Kollegen Kit Martin erwarb er 2009 die Ruine eines alten Gasthauses und setzte ein detailverliebtes Sanierungskonzept um. Mit nur acht Gästezimmern firmiert das Boutiquehotel mittlerweile als Traditional Pub. Daraus spricht britisches Understatement, eventuell sogar britischer Humor, denn obwohl die Fleischgerichte im Gunton Arms auf einem offenen Feuer gegart werden, handelt es sich bei solcher Zubereitungstechnik mittlerweile um Luxus – vor allem wenn der Chefkoch Stuart Tattersall heißt und zuvor bei Mark Hix in London-Mayfair für die Fischspezialitäten zuständig war. Der allergrößte Luxus des Gunton Arms ist aber vor der Tür des Hauses zu finden: Der Boutique Pub steht nämlich inmitten eines Naturschutzgebietes von 400 Hektar, wo sich auf nebelumflorten Wiesen nicht nur Fuchs und Hase, sondern auch Eule, Reh und Hirsch Gute Nacht sagen. Insgesamt 800 Hirsche und Rehe übrigens. All dies ist aus den traditionell mit allem Komfort eingerichteten Zimmern des Hauses zu beobachten, aus einem samtgepolsterten Ohrensessel beispielsweise. Oder man legt seufzend die Gummistiefel an und stapft über die taufeuchten Wiesen gen Abendrot. Nicht nur Wild und Natur sind in der Parklandschaft zu finden, sondern auch Skulpturen von Sol LeWitt, Anthony Caro und Dan Graham. Unter anderen. In den Speisezimmern des Gunton Arms, übrigens auch bei den Einwohnern des malerischen Umlandes beliebt, hängen Werke von Damien Hirst und Tracey Emin. Selbst an einer Wand in der Herrentoilette findet sich eine Arbeit von Araki. Gelungenes Understatement wird in Großbritannien nach wie vor gerne gesehen: Im Jahr 2013 wurde das Gunton Arms vom „Guide Michelin" zum Pub of the Year gewählt. ◆ Buchtipp: „Jane Eyre" von Charlotte Brontë.

ANREISE 255 km nördlich von London-Heathrow, 25 Min. vom Flughafen Norwich · **PREIS** €€ · **ZIMMER** 8 Zimmer, 2 Wohnzimmer (stamp rooms), die nur für Hotelgäste bestimmt sind · **KÜCHE** Regional und saisonal · **GESCHICHTE** Das ehemalige Pförtnerhaus zu einer Parklandschaft, die im 18. Jahrhundert angelegt wurde, eröffnete 2011 für Hotel- und Pubgäste · **X-FAKTOR** Englisches Landleben und zeitgenössische Kunst

L'ART DE VIVRE BUCOLIQUE

Avec le Gunton Arms, le marchand d'art Ivor Braka place la barre supposée encore un peu plus haut : c'est en 2009 qu'il a acheté avec son collègue Kit Martin la ruine d'une ancienne auberge et s'y est livré à un programme de rénovation dans l'amour du moindre détail. Avec seulement huit chambres, le boutique-hôtel se présente aujourd'hui comme un Traditional Pub. L'art britannique de l'euphémisme, voire l'humour british, y est cultivé car, si la viande du Gunton Arms est cuite directement au feu de bois, ce mode de préparation est devenu un luxe — surtout lorsque le chef porte le nom de Stuart Tattersall et a été auparavant responsable des spécialités de poisson chez Mark Hix, dans le quartier londonien de Mayfair. Mais le plus grand luxe du Gunton Arms se trouve devant la porte : le boutique-pub est situé au cœur d'un parc naturel de 400 hectares aux prairies voilées de brume où renards et lièvres, mais aussi hiboux, chevreuils et cerfs viennent le soir saluer les hôtes. Et ils sont nombreux : on compte par exemple quelque 800 cerfs et chevreuils. Le tout à observer depuis les chambres traditionnelles aménagées avec tout le confort de la maison, par exemple dans un fauteuil à oreilles aux coussins de velours. On peut aussi mettre en soupirant ses bottes en caoutchouc et marcher à travers prés dans l'herbe humide de rosée au coucher du soleil. Le gibier et la nature ne seront pas les seules rencontres dans les prairies du parc à l'anglaise, on y trouve aussi des sculptures de Sol LeWitt, Anthony Caro et Dan Graham. Et d'autres encore. Dans les salles à manger du Gunton Arms, également appréciées des habitants de cette campagne pittoresque, sont accrochées des œuvres de Damien Hirst et Tracey Emin. Et même au mur des toilettes pour hommes, on trouve un Araki. Aujourd'hui comme hier, l'euphémisme réussi est bien vu en Grande-Bretagne et, en 2013, le Gunton Arms a été nommé Pub of the Year par le Guide Michelin. ◆ À lire : « Jane Eyre » de Charlotte Brontë.

ACCÈS À 255 km au nord de l'aéroport London Heathrow, à 25 min de l'aéroport de Norwich · **PRIX** €€ · **CHAMBRES** 8 chambres, 2 salons (stamp rooms) réservés aux clients de l'hôtel · **RESTAURATION** Cuisine régionale de saison · **HISTOIRE** Ancienne loge du concierge d'un parc paysager aménagé au XVIIIe siècle, l'hôtel et pub a ouvert en 2011 · **LES « PLUS »** La vie champêtre à l'anglaise, au milieu de l'art contemporain

THE OLD
RAILWAY STATION

PETWORTH, WEST SUSSEX, ENGLAND

THE OLD
RAILWAY STATION

Petworth, West Sussex GU28 0JF, England
Tel: + 44 1798 342 346 · info@old-station.co.uk
www.old-station.co.uk

ALL ABOARD

Trains never arrive or depart on time, or indeed at any time, at this station. You can stay at The Old Railway Station without worrying about timetables and schedules, cocooned in a motion-less carriage overlooking the pretty garden. Trains once went through here on their way to and from Midhurst and Pulborough and on to London. Now the only ones left are Alicant, Mimosa, Flora and Montana, four Pullman carriages dating from 1912, 1914 and two from 1923 that have been beautifully restored into eight spacious and elegant rooms, all with en-suite bathrooms. Bearing little resemblance to their previous life as dining and parlor cars, the carriages, with their luxurious beds, plush furnishings, and soft colors, are a clever conversion of old to new. Appropriately, they are located next to the historic Victorian railway station, originally built in 1892 for the Prince of Wales, later Edward VII. Guests can choose to stay in the carriages or in either of two bedrooms in an annex to the station, whose former waiting room is now a splendid lounge for guests. There is no waiting on a drafty platform or missed connections here, just old-fashioned peace and quiet. A treasure trove of antiques is in the local village. ◆ Book to pack: "Stamboul Train" by Graham Greene.

DIRECTIONS *84 km/52 miles south of London, 30 minutes drive north of Chichester* · RATES *€€* · ROOMS *8 rooms on board, 2 in the station* · FOOD *A 5-minute walk to award-winning local pub, The Badgers Inn, for lunch and dinner* · HISTORY *The railway station was built in 1892* · X-FACTOR *Living in a grown-up's train set*

ALLE AN BORD

An diesem alten Bahnhof kommen die Züge weder pünktlich an noch fahren sie pünktlich ab, denn hier fährt überhaupt kein Zug mehr. Sorgen Sie sich also nicht um Fahrpläne und Abfahrtszeiten, sondern genießen Sie unbeschwert Ihren Aufenthalt in The Old Railway Station, in einem der stillgelegten Eisenbahnwaggons mit Blick auf den bezaubernden Garten. Denn von den Zügen, die hier früher auf dem Weg nach London und Brighton hielten, haben zwei Wurzeln geschlagen: „Alicante" und „Mimosa", zwei Pullman-Wagen aus der Zeit vor dem Ersten Weltkrieg, die liebevoll restauriert wurden und jetzt acht geräumige und elegante Zimmer beherbergen, von denen jedes mit einem Bad ausgestattet ist. Ihre Vergangenheit als Speisewagen sieht man diesen stilvoll eingerichteten Waggons mit ihren luxuriösen Betten und geschmackvoll abgestimmten Farben nicht mehr an. Sinnigerweise wurden sie direkt neben dem historischen viktorianischen Bahnhof platziert, wo die Gäste wahlweise auch in einem der zwei Zimmer im Anbau des Bahnhofs Quartier nehmen können, dessen Wartesaal zu einem romantischen Empfangsraum umgebaut wurde. Vergessen Sie lange Wartezeiten auf zugigen Bahnsteigen und verpasste Anschlusszüge. Hier finden Sie Ruhe und Frieden in nostalgischem Ambiente. Das Örtchen Petworth ist eine Fundgrube für Antiquitätenliebhaber. ◆ Buchtipp: „Orient-Express" von Graham Greene.

ANREISE *84 km südlich von London, 30 Autominuten nördlich von Chichester* · **PREIS** *€€* · **ZIMMER** *8 Zimmer „an Bord", 2 im Bahnhof* · **KÜCHE** *In 5 Gehminuten erreichen Sie den preisgekrönten Pub The Badgers Inn (Mittag- und Abendessen)* · **GESCHICHTE** *1892 wurde der Bahnhof erbaut* · **X-FAKTOR** *Eisenbahn-Spielen für Erwachsene*

FERMEZ LES PORTIÈRES

Dans cette ancienne gare, les trains n'arrivent ni ne partent jamais à l'heure : en fait, l'heure n'existe plus. À l'hôtel The Old Railway Station, vous séjournerez confortablement dans un wagon désormais immobile, avec vue sur un ravissant jardin, sans avoir à vous soucier d'horaires ou d'agendas. Les trains reliant Londres à Brighton passaient ici autrefois. Aujourd'hui, il n'en reste plus que deux wagons, Alicante et Mimosa. Ces voitures pullmans d'avant la Première Guerre mondiale, magnifiquement restaurées, abritent désormais quatre chambres spacieuses et élégantes, chacune équipée d'une salle de bains. Judicieusement converties, avec leurs lits luxueux, leur ameublement somptueux et leur décor aux couleurs douces, elles ne gardent aucune trace de leur ancienne fonction de wagon-restaurant. Elles sont stationnées, comme il convient, à côté de la gare datant de l'époque victorienne. On peut loger dans les voitures ou dans les chambres aménagées dans une annexe de la gare dont l'ancienne salle d'attente est aujourd'hui un splendide salon. Ici, tout est calme et repos. Personne n'attend de train dans les courants d'air d'un quai ni ne court pour éviter de manquer sa correspondance. Au village, des trésors attendent les amateurs d'antiquités. ◆ À lire : « Orient-Express » de Graham Greene.

ACCÈS *À 84 km au sud de Londres, à 30 min de route au nord de Chichester* · **PRIX** *€€* · **CHAMBRES** *8 chambres dans les voitures, 2 dans la gare* · **RESTAURATION** *À 5 min à pied d'un pub primé, le Badgers Inn (repas de midi et du soir)* · **HISTOIRE** *La gare existe depuis 1892* · **LES « PLUS »** *Séjour dans un train nostalgique*

THE BUNKERS

KNOKKE-HEIST, BELGIUM

THE BUNKERS

Burkeldijk 18, 8300 Knokke-Heist, Belgium
Tel. + 32 476 70 72 73 · hello@thebunkers.be
www.thebunkers.be

WIDE-OPEN SPACES

This Belgian coastal landscape behind its dikes has had an eventful, fateful history: in 1785 Joseph II of Austria, who then ruled Flanders, ordered construction of the fortress of Hazegras to protect the polder dikes and sluices that had just been built. During the First and Second World Wars, German forces occupied the terrain, which was now used for farming – and five stone bunkers remain as silent witnesses to those days. Today the residents of The Bunkers are fortunately much more peaceful: sheep, hens and bees live around the ruins, and the farm has been turned into an extremely stylish bed & breakfast by Axel De Bisscop, who grew up nearby, and his wife Margaux Corman. With the help of the Govaert & Vanhoutte architectural practice from Bruges and the interior designers Anversa from Antwerp, they combined the historic stone walls of the main house and the barn with modern facades, some of them mobile, of afromosia wood and with tall glass fronts, linked the two buildings with an underground passage, and gave the rooms minimalistic furnishings in shades of black, gray and white. A showpiece in the house is the kitchen, with massive counters, designer cupboards by Vipp and raised seating at windows that provide a superb view. From the indoor pool, glistening jade green, there is also a far-ranging view of the countryside. The sea and the fashionable beach resort of Knokke are only a few minutes away. Many guests are attracted to the chic beach bars and boutiques there. Style and peace – sometimes you simply don't need anything else. ◆ Book to pack: "The Life of the Bee" by Maurice Maeterlinck.

DIRECTIONS *Knokke is on the Belgian coast close to the border with the Netherlands, 130 km/80 miles from Brussels airport* · RATES *€€* · ROOMS *5 rooms, all with en-suite bathroom* · FOOD *There is an extensive breakfast buffet. During the day and in the evening, guests can cook for themselves or eat out in Knokke* · HISTORY *This bed & breakfast opened in December 2017* · X-FACTOR *An architectural masterpiece!*

EIN WEITES FELD

Es ist eine wechsel- und unheilvolle Geschichte, die diese Deich-landschaft an der Küste Belgiens hinter sich hat: 1785 ließ Joseph II. von Österreich, damals Herrscher über Flandern, hier die Festungs-anlage Hazegras errichten, um die gerade geschaffenen Polder-deiche und -schleusen zu schützen. Während des Ersten und Zweiten Weltkrieges hielten die Deutschen das inzwischen von Bauern genutzte Gelände besetzt – fünf Steinbunker sind stumme Zeugen dieser Zeit. Heute beherbergen „The Bunkers" glücklicher-weise weitaus friedlichere Bewohner: Rund um die Bunkerruinen leben Schafe, Hühner und Bienen; und aus dem Hof haben Axel De Bisscop, der ganz in der Nähe aufwuchs, und seine Frau Margaux Corman ein sehr stilvolles Bed & Breakfast gemacht. Mithilfe des Brügger Architekturbüros Govaert & Vanhoutte und des Innenausstatters Anversa aus Antwerpen kombinierten sie die historischen Steinmauern von Haupthaus und Scheune mit modernen, teilweise mobilen Fassaden aus Afromosia-Holz sowie mit hohen Glasfronten, verbanden beide Gebäude mit einer unterirdischen Passage und richteten die Räume minimalistisch in schwarzen, grauen und weißen Nuancen ein. Ein Schmuckstück des Hauses ist die Küche mit mächtigem Tresen, Designschränken von Vipp und Logenplätzen entlang der Fenster, die eine grandiose Aussicht eröffnen. Auch vom jadegrün schimmernden Innenpool blickt man weit über die Natur. Das Meer und das mondäne Seebad Knokke sind nur ein paar Minuten entfernt, doch viele Gäste zieht es gar nicht in die schicken Strandbars und Boutiquen. Stil und Stille – mehr ist manchmal einfach nicht nötig. ◆ Buchtipp: „Das Leben der Bienen" von Maurice Maeterlinck.

ANREISE *Knokke liegt an der belgischen Küste, nahe der Grenze zu den Niederlanden und 130 km vom Flughafen Brüssel entfernt ·* PREIS *€€ ·* ZIMMER *5 Zimmer, alle mit eigenem Bad ·* KÜCHE *Morgens gibt es ein reichhaltiges Frühstücksbuffet. Tagsüber und abends kann man selbst kochen oder in Knokke ausgehen ·* GESCHICHTE *Das Bed & Breakfast wurde im Dezember 2017 eröffnet ·* X-FAKTOR *Eine architektonische Glanzleistung!*

GRAND ANGLE

Ce paysage de digues sur la côte belge a une histoire mouvemen-tée et funeste : en 1785, l'empereur d'Autriche Joseph II, qui régnait sur les Flandres à l'époque, fit construire le fort Hazegras pour pro-téger les nouvelles digues et les écluses des polders. Pendant la Première et la Seconde Guerre mondiale, les Allemands ont occupé le site aujourd'hui utilisé par les agriculteurs – cinq bunkers en pierre sont les témoins silencieux de cette époque. Heureusement, à l'heure actuelle, les « Bunkers » abritent des habitants beaucoup plus paisibles : des moutons, des poulets et des abeilles vivent autour des ruines, et Axel De Bisscop, qui a grandi à proximité, et son épouse Margaux Corman ont transformé la ferme en un bed & breakfast très élégant. Avec l'aide du cabinet d'architectes bru-geois Govaert & Vanhoutte et de l'architecte d'intérieur anversois Anversa, ils ont combiné les murs historiques en pierre de la maison principale et de la grange avec des façades modernes et partielle-ment mobiles revêtues d'un bardage en afrormosia. Ils ont aussi ouvert de hautes baies en verre, relié les deux bâtiments par un passage souterrain et décoré les pièces de manière minimaliste avec des nuances de noir, gris et blanc. Un joyau de la maison est la cuisine qui abrite un grand comptoir, des armoires design Vipp et, le long des fenêtres, des places de choix offrant une vue grandiose sur l'extérieur. De la piscine d'intérieur vert jade scintil-lante, la vue sur le paysage alentour est imprenable. La mer et Knokke la sophistiquée ne sont qu'à quelques minutes, mais de nombreux clients ne sont pas attirés par les bars et les boutiques chic de la plage. Style et silence – parfois, il n'est tout simplement pas nécessaire d'en faire plus. ◆ À lire : « La Vie des abeilles » de Maurice Maeterlinck.

ACCÈS *Knokke est situé sur la côte belge, à la frontière avec les Pays-Bas et à 130 km de l'aéroport de Bruxelles ·* PRIX *€€ ·* CHAMBRES *5 chambres avec salle de bains ·* RESTAURATION *Buffet riche et varié pour le petit déjeuner. Pendant la journée et le soir on peut faire la cuisine soi-même ou aller à Knokke ·* HISTOIRE *Le bed & breakfast a ouvert ses portes en décembre 2017 ·* LES « PLUS » *Un exploit remarquable sur le plan architectural !*

AUGUST

ANTWERP, BELGIUM

AUGUST

Jules Bordetstraat 5, 2018 Antwerp, Belgium
Tel. + 32 3 500 80 80 · welcome@august-antwerp.com
www.august-antwerp.com

A MODERN RETREAT

This Augustinian convent in the heart of Antwerp was once the home of nuns who looked after wounded soldiers in the nearby military hospital, finding space and peace for prayer here after their labors caring for the sick. Today the five neoclassical buildings with designated heritage status accommodate one of the city's newest design hotels: August, the first hotel project by the Belgian architect Vincent Van Duysen. With great respect for the old building fabric and Flemish architecture, he has preserved the simplicity and tranquillity of this former place of retreat, at the same time providing modern features. Thus black metal elements contrast effectively with the classically white interior, and tall windows admit lots of light into rooms that were once closed-off. Van Duysen has designed many accessories exclusively for August in collaboration with well-known brands: the low-key bar and lounge furniture in the former chapel are by Molteni, the lamps by Flos, the hotel's own tableware by Serax. For the restaurant in the conservatory, the chef Nick Bril from the neighbouring Michelin-starred restaurant The Jane has composed a menu with international inspiration. And in the esthetic rooms, suites and the atelier with its loft character, guests find Egyptian bed linen, tiles from Italy and hand-woven carpets from Portugal. For chilling out there are three convent gardens, beautiful oases laid out by the Antwerp landscape gardener Wirtz, and a spa with a sauna, a hammam and an outdoor pool. ◆ Book to pack: "A Dog of Flanders" by Ouida (Maria Louise Ramé).

DIRECTIONS *Situated in the Green Quarter (Het Groen Kwartier) of Antwerp, 3 km/2 miles from Antwerp airport, 41 km/25 miles from Brussels airport* · **RATES** *€€* · **ROOMS** *44 rooms and suites* · **FOOD** *The modern brasserie serves creative seasonal treats* · **HISTORY** *Opened as a design hotel in April 2019* · **X-FACTOR** *The August Shop with a useful takeaway range (coffee, juice, salads and sandwiches)*

EIN MODERNES REFUGIUM

Einst lebten in diesem Augustinerkloster im Herzen von Antwerpen Nonnen, die sich im nahen Militärhospital um verwundete Soldaten kümmerten und hier nach der kräftezehrenden Krankenpflege Raum und Ruhe zum Gebet fanden. Heute beherbergen die fünf denkmalgeschützten, neoklassizistischen Gebäude eines der jüngsten Designhotels der Stadt, das August – erstes Hotelprojekt des belgischen Architekten Vincent Van Duysen. Mit viel Respekt für die alte Substanz und flämische Baukunst hat er Schlichtheit und Stille des ehemaligen Rückzugsortes bewahrt, aber zugleich für moderne Akzente gesorgt. So setzen sich schwarze Metallelemente wirkungsvoll vom klassisch weißen Interieur ab, und hohe Fenster lassen viel Licht in die einstmals abgeschotteten Räume. Viele Accessoires hat Van Duysen exklusiv für das August gemeinsam mit bekannten Marken entworfen: Die dezenten Bar- und Loungemöbel in der früheren Kapelle stammen von Molteni, die Lampen von Flos, die hoteleigene Tischware von Serax. Für das Restaurant im Wintergarten komponierte Starkoch Nick Bril vom benachbarten Sternerestaurant The Jane eine international inspirierte Karte. Und in den ästhetischen Zimmern, Suiten und dem loftähnlichen „Atelier" finden sich Bettwäsche aus Ägypten, Fliesen aus Italien sowie handgewebte Teppiche aus Portugal. Die Seele baumeln lassen kann man in den drei Klostergärten (von den Landschaftsarchitekten Wirtz aus Antwerpen als wunderschöne Oasen angelegt) und im Spa, das eine Sauna, einen Hamam sowie einen Außenpool umfasst. ◆ Buchtipp: „Ein Hund aus Flandern" von Ouida (Maria Louise Ramé).

ANREISE *Im „Grünen Viertel" (Het Groen Kwartier) von Antwerpen gelegen, 3 km vom Flughafen Antwerpen, 41 km vom Flughafen Brüssel entfernt ·* PREIS *€€ ·* ZIMMER *44 Zimmer und Suiten ·* KÜCHE *Die moderne Brasserie bietet saisonale, kreative Köstlichkeiten ·* GESCHICHTE *Im April 2019 als Designhotel eröffnet ·* X-FAKTOR *Der August Shop mit praktischem Take-away (Kaffee, Säfte, Salate und Sandwiches)*

UN REFUGE MODERNE

Des religieuses vivaient autrefois dans ce monastère augustinien situé au cœur d'Anvers, elles soignaient des soldats blessés dans l'hôpital militaire voisin et trouvaient ici l'espace et la paix nécessaires pour prier après ce travail épuisant. Aujourd'hui, les cinq bâtiments néoclassiques classés abritent l'August, un des plus récents hôtels design de la ville – le premier projet hôtelier de l'architecte belge Vincent Van Duysen. Avec un grand respect pour la substance ancienne et l'architecture flamande, il a su préserver la simplicité et la tranquillité de l'ancienne retraite, tout en créant des accents modernes. Ainsi, des éléments métalliques noirs se démarquent efficacement de l'intérieur blanc classique et les grandes fenêtres laissent entrer des flots de lumière dans les espaces autrefois confinés. Van Duysen a conçu de nombreux accessoires exclusivement pour l'August en collaboration avec des marques renommées : le mobilier discret du bar et du salon dans l'ancienne chapelle est de Molteni, les lampes de Flos et la vaisselle de l'hôtel est signée Serax. Et Nick Bril, le cuisinier star du restaurant étoilé voisin The Jane, a composé un menu d'inspiration internationale pour le restaurant situé dans le jardin d'hiver. Dans les chambres à la décoration recherchée, les suites et l'« Atelier » semblable à un loft, on trouve du linge de lit égyptien, des carreaux italiens et des tapis portugais tissés à la main. Détente assurée dans les trois jardins du monastère (conçus comme de magnifiques oasis par les architectes paysagistes Wirtz d'Anvers) et dans le spa, qui comprend un sauna, un hammam et une piscine extérieure. ◆ À lire : « Un chien des Flandres » de Maria Louise Ramé, dite Ouida.

ACCÈS *Dans « Le Quartier vert » (Het Groen Kwartier) d'Anvers, à 3 km de l'aéroport, à 41 km de l'aéroport de Bruxelles ·* PRIX *€€ ·* CHAMBRES *44 chambres et suites ·* RESTAURATION *La brasserie moderne propose de délicieux plats créatifs de saison ·* HISTOIRE *L'hôtel design a ouvert ses portes en avril 2019 ·* LES « PLUS » *L'August Shop avec ses plats et boissons à emporter si pratiques (café, jus de fruits, salades et sandwichs)*

SEVERIN'S RESORT & SPA

SYLT, SCHLESWIG-HOLSTEIN, GERMANY

SEVERIN'S RESORT & SPA

Am Tipkenhoog 18, 25980 Keitum, Sylt, Germany
Tel. + 49 4651 46 06 60 · info@severins-sylt.de
www.severins-sylt.de

A SYLT BEAUTY

Seen from a bird's-eye view, the main building of Severin's Resort & Spa looks like an outsized S – and has the largest continuous thatched roof in Europe, at 5,000 square metres. The reed thatching covers a building in which luxurious rooms and suites, fitted out with natural materials, await hotel guests. The spa suites with their own sauna and the maisonette suites, which are perfect for families, are especially attractive. These exclusive facilities are complemented by the surrounding apartments and villas, whose occupants can choose between hotel services and self-catering. The heart of the hotel is an award-winning spa in which all treatments are guided by the "Sylt power compass" and take advantage of the soothing influences of the island's natural world – of the sun, wind and water. Here it is easy to spend entire stress-free days of holiday enjoying holistic treatments with seaweed, sea salt or plant-based oils. In a wonderfully relaxed mood, guests can then appreciate authentic Sylt specialities in the classical Hoog restaurant for lunch and fine cuisine in the modern Tipken's for dinner, and round off a wonderful day of wellness at the bar with its open fire. ◆ Book to pack: "Sylt Novella" by Theodor Storm.

DIRECTIONS *In pretty Keitum on the east side of the island, 6 km from Westerland (for the airport and car embarkation point)* · **RATES** *€€€–€€€€* · **ROOMS** *62 rooms and suites in the main building, 22 apartments, 5 villas* · **FOOD** *In addition to two restaurants, a bar and lounge, the resort has an extremely well-stocked wine cellar, which can be booked for exclusive use at private events* · **HISTORY** *Opened in December 2014* · **X-FACTOR** *The loveliest and most stylish spa on Sylt*

SYLTER SCHÖNHEIT

Wer das Haupthaus des Severin's Resort & Spa aus der Vogel-perspektive betrachtet, sieht ein überdimensionales „S" – und das mit 5000 Quadratmetern größte zusammenhängende Reetdach Europas. Das Schilfrohr schützt ein im traditionellen friesischen Stil errichtetes Gebäude, in dem luxuriöse, mit Naturmaterialien ausgestattete Zimmer und Suiten auf Gäste warten – besonders schön sind die Spa-Suiten mit eigener Sauna sowie die Maisonette-Suiten, die sich perfekt für Familien eignen. Ergänzt wird das exklusive Angebot durch die umliegenden Apartments und Villen, deren Bewohner zwischen Hotelservices und Selbstversorgung wählen können. Das Herz des Hauses ist das preisgekrönte Spa, in dem alle Anwendungen nach dem „Sylter Kräftekompass" ausgerichtet sind und die wohltuende Wirkung der Inselnatur, von Sonne, Wind und Wasser nutzen. Hier lassen sich bei ganzheit-lichen Behandlungen mit Algen, Meersalz oder pflanzlichen Ölen mühelos und stressfrei ganze Urlaubstage verbringen. Herrlich entspannt genießt man mittags typische Sylter Spezialitäten im klassischen „Hoog" und abends die feine Küche des modernen „Tipken's" und lässt dann einen wunderbaren Wellnesstag an der Kaminbar ausklingen. ◆ Buchtipp: „Sylter Novelle" von Theodor Storm. „Falscher Glanz" von Eva Ehley (spielt z. T. im Hotel; nur auf Deutsch erhältlich)

ANREISE *Im hübschen Ort Keitum auf der Ostseite der Insel gelegen, 6 km von Westerland (Flughafen und Autoverladestelle) entfernt* · **PREIS** *€€€–€€€€* · **ZIMMER** *62 Zimmer und Suiten im Haupthaus, 22 Apartments, 5 Villen* · **KÜCHE** *Neben 2 Restaurants, einer Bar und Lounge besitzt das Resort einen sehr gut sortierten Weinkeller, der für private Events exklusiv gebucht werden kann* · **GESCHICHTE** *Im Dezember 2014 eröffnet* · **X-FAKTOR** *Das schönste und stilvollste Spa auf Sylt*

LA BEAUTÉ DE SYLT

Vu du ciel, le bâtiment principal du Severin's Resort & Spa a l'air d'un « S » surdimensionné – et possède le plus grand toit de chaume continu d'Europe avec ses 5000 mètres carrés. Les tiges de roseau qui le constituent abritent un bâtiment construit dans le style traditionnel frison, dans lequel des chambres et des suites luxueuses meublées de matériaux naturels attendent les clients. Les Spa Suites avec leur propre sauna et les Maisonette Suites, parfaitement adaptées aux besoins des familles, sont particulière-ment attrayantes. L'offre exclusive est complétée par les apparte-ments et villas avoisinants, dont les résidents peuvent choisir entre les services hôteliers et le self-catering. Le cœur de la maison est le spa primé : tous les traitements sont basés sur le « Kräftekompass de Sylt » (un test de constitution) et mettent à profit les effets béné-fiques de la nature environnante, du soleil, du vent et de l'eau. Ici, vous pouvez passer des journées entières sans effort et sans stress en bénéficiant de traitements holistiques à base d'algues, de sel de mer ou d'huiles végétales. Merveilleusement détendus, vous pourrez déguster, le midi, les spécialités typiques de Sylt dans le classique « Hoog », le soir, la cuisine raffinée du « Tipken's » et enfin terminer une merveilleuse journée de bien-être près de la cheminée du bar. ◆ À lire : « Sylter Novelle » de Theodor Storm (en allemand uniquement) et « Falscher Glanz » d'Eva Ehley (se déroule en partie dans l'hôtel ; en allemand uniquement)

ACCÈS *Situé dans le joli village de Keitum à l'est de l'île, à 6 km de Westerland (aéroport et point de chargement des voitures)* · **PRIX** *€€€-€€€€* · **CHAMBRES** *62 chambres et suites dans le bâtiment principal, 22 appartements, 5 villas* · **RESTAURATION** *À côté de 2 restaurants, un bar et lounge, le Resort possède une cave à vin très bien garnie qui peut être réservée exclusivement pour des événements privés* · **HISTOIRE** *L'hôtel a ouvert ses portes en décembre 2014* · **LES « PLUS »** *Le spa le plus beau et le plus élégant de Sylt*

OLE LIESE

PANKER, SCHLESWIG-HOLSTEIN, GERMANY

OLE LIESE

Gut Panker, 24321 Panker, Germany
Tel. + 49 4381 906 90 · info@ole-liese.de
www.ole-liese.de

ON THE TRAIL OF LIESE

This country house hotel owes its existence and its name to the favorite horse of Friedrich Wilhelm von Hessenstein, a prince of the Holy Roman Empire and son of the king of Sweden – illegitimate, and therefore excluded from succession to the throne. Far from Stockholm, he lived on the estate Gut Panker in the late 18th century, and granted to one of his stable and carriage hands the licence to keep an inn, in gratitude for the man's work in looking after his faithful mare Liese in her old age. Today Gut Panker is known as a stud for Trakehner horses (30 horses live here compared to 80 human residents, and holiday guests can bring and stable their own horses here), and also as one of the prettiest inns in the region known as "Holstein's Switzerland". Ole Liese is managed by Birthe and Oliver Domnick, who once celebrated their wedding in the hotel and later, when new tenants were being sought, gave up their jobs in a luxury hotel in Hamburg in order to spoil tourists in this north German idyll. It has bright, well-kept rooms in a country-house style with a touch of Scandinavia, a cosy parlor with an open fire, a small spa zone and two outstanding restaurants – one serving rustic, regional dishes, the other with refined, award-winning gourmet menus. On foot, on a bike or in the saddle of a horse, guests can roam the fields, lakes and hilly landscape around the hotel, and "climb" the 128-meter-high Pielsberg hill. From up there, in clear weather, there is a sweeping view from the Baltic Sea across to Denmark. ◆ Book to pack: "The German Lesson" by Siegfried Lenz.

DIRECTIONS *On the edge of the Holsteinische Schweiz, close to the Baltic Sea, 100 km/63 miles north of Hamburg airport* · RATES *€–€€* · ROOMS *23 rooms and suites* · FOOD *Restaurant 1797 has a Michelin star (open from late March to early October, Wednesday to Saturday, evenings only)* · HISTORY *The history of Gut Panker goes back to the 15th century. Ole Liese was founded in 1797* · X-FACTOR *The charming hosts*

AUF LIESES SPUREN

Seine Existenz und seinen Namen verdankt dieses Landhaushotel dem Lieblingspferd des Reichsfürsten Friedrich Wilhelm von Hessenstein, einem unehelichen Sohn des schwedischen Königs und daher von der Thronfolge ausgeschlossen. Fern von Stockholm lebte er Ende des 18. Jahrhunderts auf Gut Panker und erteilte einem Reit- und Wagenknecht eine Schanklizenz als Dank dafür, dass dieser seiner treuen Stute Liese das Gnadenbrot gab. Heute ist Gut Panker als Trakehnergestüt bekannt (auf 80 Bewohner kommen hier 30 Pferde, und Feriengäste können ihr eigenes Tier mitbringen und im Stall einstellen) – und für einen der hübschesten Gasthöfe der Holsteinischen Schweiz. Pächter der „Ole Liese" sind Birthe und Oliver Domnick, die im Hotel einst ihre Hochzeit feierten und später, als neue Betreiber gesucht wurden, ihre Jobs in einem Hamburger Luxushotel aufgaben, um Touristen in diesem norddeutschen Idyll zu verwöhnen. Dazu gehören gepflegte, helle Zimmer im skandinavisch angehauchten Landhausstil, eine gemütliche Kaminhalle, ein kleiner Wellnessbereich sowie zwei hervorragende Restaurants – das eine mit rustikaler, regionaler Küche, das andere mit feinen, preisgekrönten Gourmetmenüs. Zu Fuß, auf dem Fahrrad oder beim Ausritt kann man die Rapsfelder, Seen und Hügellandschaften rund um das Hotel erkunden und den 128 Meter hohen Pielsberg „erklimmen". Bei klarem Wetter reicht die Sicht von oben weit über die Ostsee bis nach Dänemark. ◆ Buchtipp: „Deutschstunde" von Siegfried Lenz.

ANREISE *Am Rand der Holsteinischen Schweiz nahe der Ostsee gelegen, 100 km nördlich des Flughafens Hamburg* · PREIS *€–€€* · ZIMMER *23 Zimmer und Suiten* · KÜCHE *Das „Restaurant 1797" hat einen Michelin-Stern (geöffnet Ende März bis Anfang Oktober, Mittwoch bis Samstag, nur abends)* · GESCHICHTE *Die Historie von Gut Panker reicht bis ins 15. Jahrhundert zurück. Gründungsjahr des „Ole Liese" war 1797* · X-FAKTOR *Die charmanten Gastgeber*

SUR LES TRACES DE LA VIEILLE LIESE

Cet hôtel de campagne doit son existence et son nom au cheval préféré du prince d'Empire Frédéric-Guillaume de Hessenstein, fils illégitime du roi de Suède et donc exclu de la succession à la couronne. Loin de Stockholm, il vivait au manoir de Panker à la fin du XVIIIᵉ siècle et accorda une licence de débit de boisson au palefrenier qui prenait soin de sa fidèle jument Liese, en retraite bien méritée. Aujourd'hui, Gut Panker est connu pour son élevage de trakehner (il y a ici 30 chevaux pour 80 habitants, et les vacanciers peuvent amener leurs propres montures et les garder dans l'écurie) – et pour être l'un des plus beaux hôtels de cette région qu'on appelle parfois la Suisse holsteinienne. Birthe et Oliver Domnick, les gérants de l'« Ole Liese », ont célébré leur mariage dans l'hôtel. Plus tard, quand de nouveaux exploitants ont été recherchés, ils ont quitté leur emploi dans un hôtel de luxe de Hambourg pour chouchouter les touristes dans ce lieu idyllique d'Allemagne du Nord. On trouve ici des chambres claires et soignées dans le style des maisons de campagne scandinaves, une salle confortable agrémentée d'une cheminée, un petit espace réservé au bien-être et deux restaurants remarquables – l'un proposant une cuisine régionale rustique et l'autre des menus gastronomiques raffinés et primés. Vous pouvez explorer les champs de colza, les lacs et les paysages vallonnés autour de l'hôtel à pied, à cheval ou à bicyclette et « escalader » le Pielsberg (128 mètres d'altitude). Par temps clair, on voit d'ici bien au-delà de la mer Baltique jusqu'au Danemark. ◆ À lire : « La Leçon d'allemand » de Siegfried Lenz.

ACCÈS *Au bord de la Suisse holsteinienne près de la Baltique, à 100 km au nord de l'aéroport de Hambourg* · PRIX *€–€€* · CHAMBRES *23 chambres et suites* · RESTAURATION *Le « Restaurant 1797 » a une étoile au Michelin (ouvert de fin mars à début octobre, du mercredi au samedi et uniquement le soir)* · HISTOIRE *L'histoire du Gut Panker remonte au XVᵉ siècle. Le « Ole Liese » a été fondé en 1797* · LES « PLUS » *La gentillesse des hôtes*

TANNERHOF

BAYRISCHZELL, BAVARIA, GERMANY

TANNERHOF

Tannerhofstraße 32, 83735 Bayrischzell, Germany ·
Tel: + 49 8023 810 · info@tannerhof.de
www.tannerhof.de
www.natur-hotel-tannerhof.de

GOOD HEALTH!

For more than a century, the von Mengershausen family of doctors ran a sanatorium in Bayrischzell. Depending on which generation was in charge, patients' health regimes were the Kneipp cure, Buchinger's rules for fasting, or treatment for the heart and circulation. However, the classic health spa operation then went into decline, and the owners prescribed a holistic rejuvenating therapy for the Tannerhof. The Munich architect Florian Nagler renovated the main building and outbuildings, which lie in the mountains like a village, and added modern "hut towers" to the existing hermit-like "air huts" from the early days. The rooms are stacked one above the other, and the top floor is accessed via an ingenious stairway. Guests can still take a fasting cure, but the range of services in the new hotel has been extended, with massages, beauty programmes and walks, as well as medical treatments with an emphasis on health checks and nutritional advice. A few details remain as reminders of the former strict rules of the sanatorium: in the restaurant there is no à la carte menu, and the rooms have neither television nor Wi-Fi internet. To make up for this, the daily menu for all guests is truly delicious – and the hot-water bottle that is a standard feature of the rooms is sometimes worth more than high-tech in the mountains. ◆ Book to pack: "Success" by Lion Feuchtwanger.

DIRECTIONS *Located above Bayrischzell, 103 km/64 miles from Munich airport* · **RATES** *€€–€€€, with breakfast, soup and salad at midday, fixed daily menu in the evening* · **ROOMS** *56 rooms in the huts and hotel (some with very small bathrooms)* · **FOOD** *Regional and 100% organic* · **HISTORY** *Newly opened in late 2011 as a nature hotel & health resort. The alpine architecture has been awarded several prizes* · **X-FACTOR** *The bathhouse with a swimming pool, sauna and sun terrace*

GESUNDHEIT!

Länger als ein Jahrhundert führte die Arztfamilie von Mengershausen in Bayrischzell ein Sanatorium. Je nachdem, welche Generation gerade am Zug war, kurierten die Patienten auf Kneippsche Art, befolgten die Buchinger Fastenregeln oder brachten ihr Herz-Kreislauf-System in Schwung. Doch dann schwächelte der klassische Kurbetrieb, und die Besitzer verschrieben ihm eine ganzheitliche, verjüngende Therapie. Der Münchner Architekt Florian Nagler renovierte Haupt- und Nebengebäude des Tannerhofs, die wie ein Dorf in den Bergen liegen, und fügte den einsiedlerartigen „Lufthütten" aus den Anfangstagen moderne „Hüttentürme" hinzu. Deren Räume stapeln sich gleichsam übereinander, und die obere Etage ist über eine raffinierte Treppe erreichbar. Heilfasten können Gäste noch immer, doch die Servicepalette des neuen Hotels wurde um Massagen, Schönheitsprogramme, Wanderungen sowie Arztbehandlungen mit Schwerpunkten auf Gesundheitschecks und Ernährungsberatung erweitert. Ein paar Details erinnern noch an die einstmals strenge Sanatoriumsordnung: So gibt es im Restaurant keine Auswahl à la carte und in den Zimmern weder Fernseher noch kabelloses Internet. Doch dafür ist das tägliche Menü für alle wirklich köstlich – und die Wärmflasche, die in den Zimmern zum Standard zählt, erweist sich in den Bergen bisweilen hilfreicher als Hightech. ◆ Buchtipp: „Erfolg" von Lion Feuchtwanger.

ANREISE *Oberhalb von Bayrischzell gelegen, 103 km vom Flughafen München entfernt ·* **PREIS** *€€–€€€, mit Frühstück, Suppe & Salat mittags, festem Tagesmenü abends ·* **ZIMMER** *56 Zimmer in Hütten und Hotel (einige mit sehr kleinen Bädern) ·* **KÜCHE** *Regional und 100 % biologisch ·* **GESCHICHTE** *Ende 2011 als Naturhotel & Gesundheitsresort neu eröffnet. Die alpine Architektur wurde mit mehreren Preisen ausgezeichnet ·* **X-FAKTOR** *Das Badehaus mit Schwimmbad, Sauna und Sonnenterrasse*

À VOTRE SANTÉ !

Pendant plus d'un siècle, la famille de médecins von Mengershausen a dirigé un sanatorium à Bayrischzell. Au fil des générations, les patients ont guéri à la manière de Kneipp, suivi les règles du jeûne de Buchinger ou renforcé leur système cardiovasculaire. Mais l'entreprise de spa classique a commencé à montrer des signes de faiblesse et les propriétaires lui ont prescrit une thérapie holistique et rajeunissante. L'architecte munichois Florian Nagler a rénové les bâtiments principaux et annexes du Tannerhof, situé dans les montagnes comme un village, et a ajouté des « huttes-tours » modernes aux huttes d'origine que des ermites n'auraient pas reniées. Leurs pièces sont en quelque sorte empilées les unes sur les autres et l'étage supérieur est accessible par un escalier ingénieux. Jeûner pour guérir est encore possible ici, mais la gamme de services offerts par le nouvel hôtel a été étendue pour inclure des massages, des programmes de beauté, des randonnées et des traitements médicaux, l'accent étant mis sur les bilans de santé et la diététique. Quelques détails nous rappellent encore le règlement strict du sanatorium d'antan : le restaurant ne propose pas de plats à la carte et les chambres ne disposent ni de télévision ni d'Internet sans fil. Mais le soir, le menu unique est vraiment délicieux – et la bouillotte, standard dans les chambres, s'avère parfois plus utile en montagne que la haute technologie. ◆ À lire : « Erfolg » de Lion Feuchtwanger (non traduit en français).

ACCÈS *Au-dessus de Bayrischzell, à 103 km de l'aéroport de Munich ·* **PRIX** *€€–€€€. Avec petit déjeuner, soupe et salade le midi, menu journalier fixe le soir ·* **CHAMBRES** *56 chambres dans les huttes et l'hôtel (certaines disposent de très petites salles de bains) ·* **RESTAURATION** *Produits régionaux et 100 % biologiques ·* **HISTOIRE** *Réouvert fin 2011 comme Naturhotel & Gesundheitsresort (hôtel au naturel et centre de santé). L'architecture alpine a été récompensée de plusieurs prix ·* **LES « PLUS »** *La maison de bains qui abrite une piscine, un sauna et une terrasse solarium*

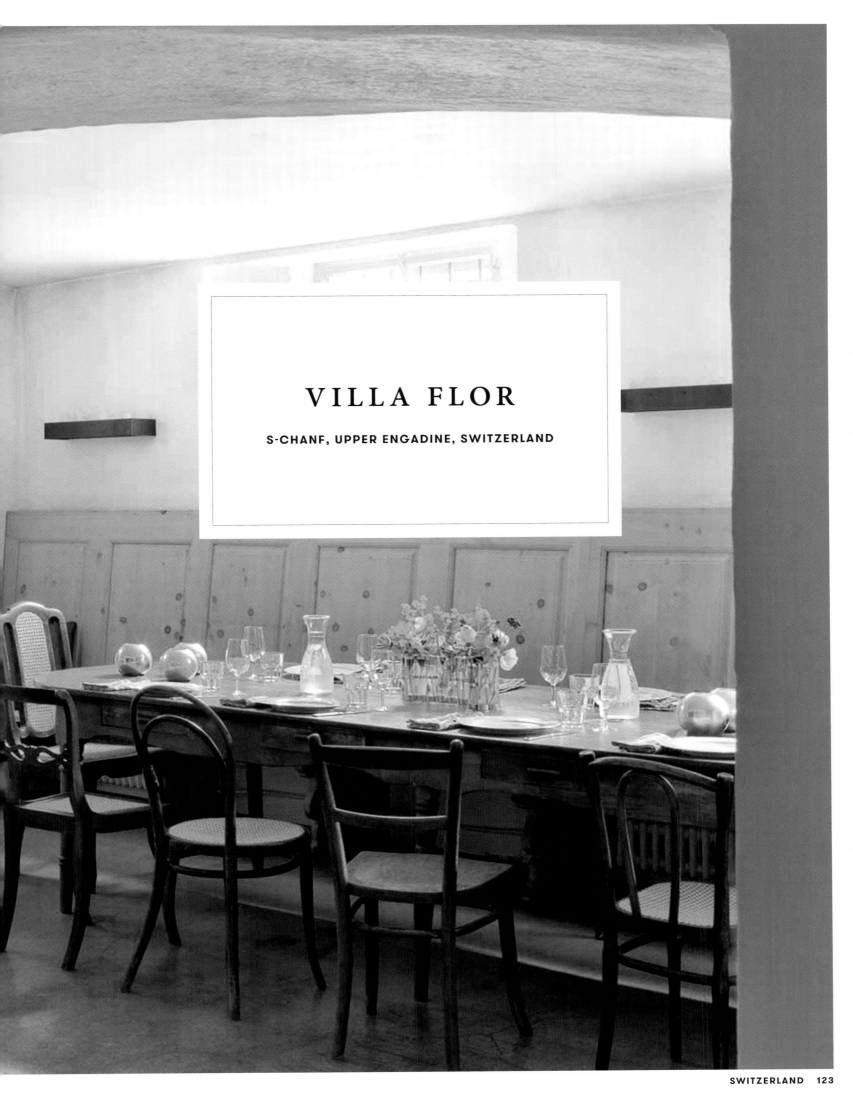

VILLA FLOR

S-CHANF, UPPER ENGADINE, SWITZERLAND

VILLA FLOR

Somvih 19, 7525 S-chanf, Switzerland
Tel. + 41 81 851 2230 · info@villaflor.ch
www.villaflor.ch
Open from mid-December to mid-April and from mid-June to mid-October

LADINA'S LIFE

They were among the Randolinas Engiadinaisas – the "Engadine swallows", who emigrated from their homeland in flocks to seek their fortune abroad. Members of the Cloetta family worked for many years in Parma in Italy, before returning home prosperous, and building this house in 1904. The present owner also flew away for a while: Ladina Florineth was a make-up artist who jetted around the world and lived out of a suitcase – until she finally landed in Switzerland again, starting out by running a gallery, and then opening Villa Flor in S-chanf. In cooperation with the architect Christian Klainguti, she carefully restored the mansion, retained the original wooden wall and ceiling panelling, polished the hundred-year-old stove and had the delicate Art Nouveau paintings rejuvenated by hand. Each of the seven rooms is furnished individually and eclectically with family heirlooms and finds from flea markets,

vintage lamps and design classics; there is a well-stocked library and an atmospheric Red Salon where the guests assemble in the evenings. All rooms and even the staircase of Villa Flor also serve as exhibition spaces. Ladina Florineth has an extensive network in the art and cultural scene, and often brings famous visitors and their works to the house. Even Julian Schnabel once made his way to the Engadine and painted the outsized picture in the reception area.
◆ Book to pack: "Autobiographical Writings" by Hermann Hesse.

DIRECTIONS *S-chanf lies at an altitude of 1,660 meters in the Upper Engadine, 21 km/13 miles from St Moritz* · **RATES** *€€* · **ROOMS** *7 rooms* · **FOOD** *A hearty breakfast with regional products is served in the mornings* · **HISTORY** *This bed & breakfast opened in 2009* · **X-FACTOR** *The first-class tips from the owner for trips and restaurants*

LADINAS LEBEN

Sie gehörten zu den „Randolinas Engiadinaisas" – den Engadiner Schwalben, die in Scharen aus ihrer Heimat auszogen, um im Ausland ihr Glück und Geld zu suchen: Die Mitglieder der Familie Cloetta arbeiteten lange Jahre im italienischen Parma, ehe sie wohlhabend nach Hause zurückkehrten und 1904 dieses Haus bauten. Auch die heutige Besitzerin flog eine Weile aus: Ladina Florineth jettete als Visagistin rund um die Welt und lebte aus dem Koffer – bis sie schließlich wieder in der Schweiz landete, als Galeristin begann und dann die Villa Flor in S-chanf eröffnete. Gemeinsam mit dem Architekten Christian Klainguti restaurierte sie das Herrschaftsgebäude sorgfältig, erhielt die originalen Wand- und Deckenvertäfelungen aus Holz, polierte die einhundert Jahre alten Öfen auf und ließ die filigranen Jugendstilmalereien von Hand auffrischen. Jedes der sieben Zimmer ist mit Familienerbstücken und Flohmarktfunden, Vintagelampen und Designklassikern individuell und eklektisch eingerichtet; es gibt eine gut sortierte Bibliothek sowie einen atmosphärischen Roten Salon, in dem die Gäste abends zusammenkommen. Sämtliche Räume und sogar das Treppenhaus der Villa Flor dienen auch als Ausstellungsfläche. Ladina Florineth ist in der Kunst- und Kulturszene weit vernetzt und bringt immer wieder berühmte Besucher und deren Werke ins Haus. Selbst Julian Schnabel fand schon einmal den Weg ins Engadin und gestaltete das überdimensionale Gemälde an der Rezeption. ◆ Buchtipp: „Engadiner Erlebnisse" von Hermann Hesse.

ANREISE *S-chanf liegt 1660 m hoch im Oberengadin, 21 km von St Moritz entfernt ·* PREIS *€€ ·* ZIMMER *7 Zimmer ·* KÜCHE *Morgens wird ein herzhaftes Frühstück mit regionalen Produkten serviert ·* GESCHICHTE *Das Bed & Breakfast wurde 2009 eröffnet ·* X-FAKTOR *Die erstklassigen Ausflugs- und Restauranttipps der Besitzerin*

LA VIE DE LADINA

Ils étaient de ces « randolinas engiadinaisas », ces hirondelles de l'Engadine, qui ont quitté leur patrie en grand nombre pour trouver le bonheur à l'étranger et faire fortune : les membres de la famille Cloetta ont travaillé pendant de nombreuses années à Parme, en Italie, ont acquis une certaine aisance, puis sont rentrés chez eux et ont construit cette maison en 1904. La propriétaire actuelle a, elle aussi, quitté le nid pendant un certain temps : Ladina Florineth a fait le tour du monde en tant que visagiste et vécu dans ses valises – jusqu'à ce qu'elle atterrisse finalement en Suisse, faisant ses débuts de galeriste avant d'ouvrir la Villa Flor à S-chanf. Avec l'architecte Christian Klainguti, elle a restauré le manoir avec soin, conservé les lambris d'origine des murs et plafonds, poli les poêles centenaires et fait rafraîchir à la main les délicates peintures Art nouveau. Chacune des sept chambres est meublée de manière individuelle et éclectique avec des objets de famille et des trouvailles chinées sur les marchés aux puces, des lampes vintage et des classiques du design ; il y a une bibliothèque bien fournie et un salon rouge chaleureux où les hôtes se retrouvent le soir. Toutes les pièces et même l'escalier de la Villa Flor servent également d'espace d'exposition. Ladina Florineth cultive ses réseaux dans le monde artistique et culturel et ne cesse de faire venir des visiteurs célèbres et leurs œuvres. Même Julian Schnabel a trouvé le chemin de l'Engadine et créé le tableau surdimensionné qui orne la réception. ◆ À lire : « Engadiner Erlebnisse » de Hermann Hesse (non traduit en français).

ACCÈS *S-chanf est situé à 1 660 m d'altitude dans la Haute Engadine, à 21 km de Saint-Moritz ·* PRIX *€€ ·* CHAMBRES *7 chambres ·* RESTAURATION *Le matin, un savoureux petit déjeuner à base de produits régionaux est servi ·* HISTOIRE *Le bed & breakfast a ouvert ses portes en 2009 ·* LES « PLUS » *Les tuyaux formidables de la propriétaire pour faire des randonnées réussies et trouver de bons restaurants*

HOTEL BELVÉDÈRE

WENGEN, BERNESE OBERLAND
SWITZERLAND

HOTEL BELVÉDÈRE

3823 Wengen, Switzerland
Tel: + 41 33 856 68 68 · hotel@belvedere-wengen.ch
www.belvedere-wengen.ch

END OF THE ROAD

No road leads here, the only way to reach this Swiss village is by mountain railway. However, there are some who won't be disheartened by this fact. If you are here in September, you can watch them run into town: as competitors in what must be one of the most gruelling marathons in the world. The runners pass through Wengen, on their way to even greater heights. In January, athletes in the Downhill Ski Racing World Cup head the opposite way. Those of us who are not in such a hurry can stay put at the Belvédère Hotel. Rather than run up or ski down the mountains, you can look out at them from the balconies. The charming hotel was built in 1912, and has retained its Art Nouveau style. It is in the center of the lively village, and skiing, hiking, and mountaineering routes are all easily accessible. As well as the great views, the advantage of the place is that there is little time wasted before setting ski to snow. This is a perfect starting point for several ski runs, most of which lead back to the village; as well as miles of ski pistes there are paths for walkers, and cable cars that take passengers to other picturesque villages. ◆ Book to pack: "The Magic Mountain" by Thomas Mann.

DIRECTIONS *Wengen is about 70 km/44 miles south of Bern. From Interlaken by rail to Lauterbrunnen and then to Wengen. The hotel is a 5-minute walk from the Wengen train station ·* RATES € · ROOMS *62 rooms ·* FOOD *Bracing classic Swiss fare served in the hotel's restaurant. Nearby is the Piz Gloria, a revolving restaurant 3,000 meters up, on the top of one of the highest peaks in Europe ·* HISTORY *The Belvédère was built in 1912 in the Art Nouveau style ·* X-FACTOR *A character hotel in a resort village that have both kept their charm*

AM ENDE DER STRASSE

Es gibt keine Straße, sondern nur eine Bergbahn, mit der Sie dieses schweizerische Dorf erreichen können. Doch einige Leute scheinen diese Tatsache zu ignorieren. Im September kann man ihnen dabei zusehen, wie sie in die Stadt rennen, genauer gesagt, wie sie an einem der anstrengendsten Marathonläufe der Welt teilnehmen. Die Läufer passieren Wengen, bevor sie noch größere Höhen erklimmen. Im Januar hingegen rasen Athleten beim World Cup im Abfahrtslauf in genau die entgegengesetzte Richtung. Wer jedoch keine solche Eile hat, kann einfach im Hotel Belvédère bleiben. Anstatt die Berge hinaufzurennen oder herabzubrettern, kann man sie vom Balkon aus einfach nur genießen. Das charmante Hotel stammt aus dem Jahr 1912; seine Jugendstil-Architektur wurde bis heute erhalten. Mitten im Zentrum des äußerst lebendigen Skiortes gelegen, lässt es sich direkt vor der Haustür natürlich auch Ski fahren, wandern oder bergsteigen. Abgesehen vom wunderschönen Panorama hat Wengen noch einen anderen großen Pluspunkt. Skiläufer müssen keine langen Wege auf sich nehmen, sondern gelangen schnell zu mehreren Pisten, von denen die meisten ins Dorf zurückführen. Außerdem gibt es Wanderwege sowie Gondeln, die sie zu anderen, nicht minder pittoresken Dörfern und wieder zurück bringen. ◆ Buchtipp: „Der Zauberberg" von Thomas Mann.

ANREISE *Wengen liegt etwa 70 km südlich von Bern. Mit dem Zug erreichen Sie Wengen von Interlaken über Lauterbrunnen. Vom Bahnhof sind es nur 5 Min. zu Fuß zum Hotel ·* PREIS € · ZIMMER *62 Zimmer ·* KÜCHE *Klassische schweizerische Küche im Hotelrestaurant. In der Nähe liegt in 3000 m Höhe, auf einem der höchsten Gipfel Europas, das Drehrestaurant Piz Gloria ·* GESCHICHTE *Das Belvédère wurde 1912 im Jugendstil erbaut ·* X-FAKTOR *Individuelles Hotel in einem Erholungsort – beide mit großem Charme*

LE BOUT DU MONDE

Il n'y a pas de route pour s'y rendre ; seul un petit train de montagne permet d'accéder à ce village suisse. Mais certains ne l'utilisent même pas : si vous séjournez ici en septembre, vous verrez une foule pressée avancer vers la ville, dans le cadre de ce qui doit être l'un des plus rudes marathons du monde. Les coureurs traversent Wengen avant de s'élancer dans les hauteurs. En janvier, les athlètes de la Coupe du monde de ski alpin dévalent dans l'autre sens. Les moins sportifs, quant à eux, choisiront de loger à l'hôtel Belvédère. Plutôt que de gravir les montagnes ou les descendre à ski, ils observeront les champions depuis leur balcon. Ce charmant hôtel de style Art nouveau, construit en 1912, est situé au centre du village animé. Il se prête à toutes les activités de montagne, ski, randonnée et alpinisme. Outre un superbe panorama, le Belvédère offre un accès direct aux pistes de ski, dont la plupart rejoignent le village. En plus des kilomètres de pistes, on trouvera également de beaux sentiers de randonnée et des téléphériques menant à d'autres localités pittoresques des environs. ◆ À lire : « La Montagne magique » de Thomas Mann.

ACCÈS *À environ 70 km au sud de Berne. En train depuis Interlaken via Lauterbrunnen ; l'hôtel est à 5 min à pied de la gare de Wengen ·* PRIX € · CHAMBRES *62 chambres ·* RESTAURATION *Le restaurant de l'hôtel sert de solides spécialités suisses. À proximité, le Piz Gloria est un restaurant panoramique situé à 3 000 m d'altitude ·* HISTOIRE *L'hôtel de style Art nouveau a été construit en 1912 ·* LES « PLUS » *Hôtel de caractère dans une station de sports d'hiver de charme*

HOTEL LOOSHAUS
AM KREUZBERG

PAYERBACH, LOWER AUSTRIA, AUSTRIA

HOTEL LOOSHAUS AM KREUZBERG

Kreuzberg 60, 2650 Payerbach, Austria
Tel: + 43 2666 52911 · steiner@looshaus.at
www.looshaus.at

NATURE, NO ORNAMENT

"Design a country house for me; rustic, but with style", might have been the brief that Paul Khuner gave the famous architect Adolf Loos. This is the house that was built for him in 1930. Loos was keen on design that was free of decoration, and explained his beliefs in an essay titled "Ornament and Crime". He argued that rich materials and good workmanship made up for a lack of decoration, and in fact far outshone it. The house may not be a decorative one, but it is not plain. Kept preserved much like it was when first built, it is now a hotel. The Hotel Looshaus am Kreuzberg is perched high on a hillside in the Austrian Alps, encircled by fresh clean mountain air. While its function has altered, the present owners have guarded its original nature, which is as it should be for a building that has been recognized as a state treasure. Although some renovation has been carried out, it is in accord with the design. The colorful interior is proof of the architect's edict that planning should be done from the inside out, and his fondness for cubic shapes is obvious. The region is famed for its winter sports and spas, as well as being home to this design jewel. ◆ Books to pack: "Ornament and Crime" by Adolf Loos and "Brother of Sleep" by Robert Schneider.

DIRECTIONS *An hour's drive south of Vienna* · RATES *€€€* · ROOMS *14 rooms* · FOOD *Home-style cooking with regional specialities* · HISTORY *Built in 1930, the Looshaus was adapted as a holiday resort at the beginning of the 1950s* · X-FACTOR *Design classic in a spectacular setting*

NATUR, KEINE ORNAMENTE

„Entwerfen Sie mir ein Landhaus, rustikal, aber mit Stil", so mag die Anweisung des Lebensmittelfabrikanten Paul Khuner an den berühmten Architekten Adolf Loos gelautet haben. Das Ergebnis ist dieses 1930 erbaute Haus. Loos war Verfechter eines geradlinigen, schnörkellosen Stils, der seine Philosophie in einem Essay mit dem vielsagenden Titel „Ornament und Verbrechen" erläuterte. Seiner Meinung nach waren hochwertige Materialien und handwerkliches Können weitaus wichtiger als dekorative Elemente. Und so ist dieses zweigeschossige Blockhaus, das bei seiner Umgestaltung zu dem heutigen Hotel weitgehend im Originalzustand belassen wurde, auch nicht überschwänglich ausgeschmückt, dabei jedoch alles andere als schlicht. Das Hotel Looshaus am Kreuzberg liegt an einem Berghang hoch in den österreichischen Alpen, umgeben von frischer, reiner Bergluft. Obwohl es seine Funktion geändert hat, haben die heutigen Besitzer es originalgetreu renoviert, wie es

einem Gebäude angemessen ist, das als nationales Baudenkmal anerkannt wurde. Notwendige Renovierungsarbeiten erfolgten in engem Einklang mit dem ursprünglichen Design. Die farbenfrohen Interieurs sind der beste Beweis dafür, dass ein Haus von innen nach außen geplant werden sollte, so wie es der Architekt forderte, und zeugen von seiner Liebe zu kubischen Formen. Abgesehen von diesem architektonischen Juwel ist die Region berühmt für ihr Wintersportangebot und ihre Kurorte. ◆ Buchtipps: „Ornament und Verbrechen" von Adolf Loos und „Schlafes Bruder" von Robert Schneider.

ANREISE *1 Std. mit dem Auto südlich von Wien* · **PREIS** *€€€* · **ZIMMER** *14 Zimmer* · **KÜCHE** *Berühmte Hausmannskost mit regionalen Spezialitäten* · **GESCHICHTE** *1930 erbaut und Anfang der 1950er-Jahre zum Hotel umgebaut* · **X-FAKTOR** *Designklassiker in spektakulärer Umgebung*

NATURE SANS ORNEMENTS

« Dessinez-moi une maison de campagne, rustique, mais qui ait du style ! » Telle aurait pu être la commande passée par Paul Khuner au célèbre architecte Adolf Loos, et telle est la maison construite pour lui en 1930. Loos préconisait une architecture dépouillée et a exposé ses principes dans un manifeste intitulé « Ornement et Crime ». Il affirmait que la richesse des matériaux et la qualité du travail compensaient l'absence de décoration, qu'en fait, ces deux facteurs jouaient un rôle bien plus important. Si la maison n'est pas décorative, elle sort cependant de l'ordinaire. Transformée en hôtel, elle conserve en grande partie son état d'origine. L'hôtel Looshaus am Kreuzberg, perché à flanc de montagne dans les Alpes autrichiennes, respire l'air frais alpin. Bien qu'il ait changé de fonction, ses propriétaires actuels ont veillé à lui garder son aspect original, comme il se doit pour un bâtiment classé. Les quelques

rénovations effectuées s'accordent avec la conception d'origine. L'aménagement aux couleurs vives illustre parfaitement la prédilection de l'architecte pour les formes cubiques et son principe selon lequel la conception devait se faire de l'intérieur. Au-delà de ce bijou d'architecture, la région est réputée pour ses stations de sports d'hiver et ses villes d'eau. ◆ À lire : « Frère sommeil » de Robert Schneider.

ACCÈS *À 1 h de route au sud de Vienne* · **PRIX** *€€€* · **CHAMBRES** *14 chambres* · **RESTAURATION** *Cuisine familiale réputée avec spécialités régionales* · **HISTOIRE** *Construit en 1930, le Looshaus a été transformé en hôtel au début des années 1950* · **LES « PLUS »** *Design classique dans un cadre spectaculaire*

DER SEEHOF

GOLDEGG AM SEE, SALZBURG COUNTRY, AUSTRIA

DER SEEHOF

Hofmark 8, 5622 Goldegg am See, Austria
Tel: + 43 6415 81 37 0 · office@derseehof.at
www.derseehof.at

ART BY THE LAKE

Even critical editors-in-chief and demanding writers have enthused about the Seehof: one wrote of an "enchantment facility", a second that "people who don't live here understand nothing about life", and a third concluded "I am more at home at the Seehof than when I am at home". With great sensitivity to culture, art and culinary matters, Susi and Sepp Schellhorn have created a special place that they regard more as a house for friends than as a hotel. The idea is that their guests should slow down, relax in themed rooms by artists and designers, find their favorite literature in the library with its complete set of first editions from the publisher Suhrkamp, and take inspiration from the modern original paintings that hang all over the house (the collection, including treasures by Gerhard Richter and Maria Lassnig, among others, is larger than the available wall space). In the open kitchen of the Hecht r120 restaurant, guests can watch as the chef conjures new interpretations of recipes from an old family cookbook. The "r120"

supplement to the name signifies that almost all products come from within a radius of 120 km/75 miles. The sources closest to the kitchen are the Seehof's own vegetable garden and the Moorsee lake, from which guests can catch their own fish for dinner. The lake is among the finest accessories of the house, especially in summer, when the water reaches temperatures of up to 26 degrees Celsius. ◆ Book to pack: "Gathering Evidence" by Thomas Bernhard.

DIRECTIONS *In an idyllic site on the lake Goldegger See in the Pongau region, 60 km/37 miles from Salzburg airport* · **RATES** *€€–€€€* · **ROOMS** *22 rooms and 5 suites* · **FOOD** *The creative regional cuisine regularly gets an award from Gault&Millau* · **HISTORY** *The oldest part of the Seehof date from 1727. Susi and Sepp Schellhorn are the fifth generation to run the family business* · **X-FACTOR** *Regular readings, often with actors from the Burgtheater in Vienna*

KUNST AM SEE

Selbst kritische Chefredakteure und anspruchsvolle Schriftsteller gerieten im Seehof ins Schwärmen: Von einer „Verzauberungsanstalt" schrieb einer. „Wer hier nicht lebt, versteht nichts vom Leben", befand ein zweiter, und „Im Seehof bin ich mehr daheim als daheim", resümierte ein dritter. Mit viel Sinn für Kultur, Kunst und Kulinarik haben Susi und Sepp Schellhorn einen ganz besonderen Ort geschaffen, den sie mehr als ein Haus für Freunde als ein Hotel verstehen. Entschleunigen soll man bei ihnen, in den von Künstlern und Designern entworfenen Themenzimmern entspannen, in der Bibliothek mit sämtlichen Suhrkamp-Erstausgaben neue Lieblingsliteratur finden und sich von den modernen Originalgemälden überall im Haus inspirieren lassen (die Sammlung mit Schätzen unter anderem von Gerhard Richter und Maria Lassnig ist schon größer als die verfügbare Wandfläche). In der offenen Küche des Restaurants Hecht r120 können Gäste dem Koch zu sehen, wie er Rezepte aus dem alten Familienkochbuch neu interpretiert. Der Zusatz „r120" steht dafür, dass fast alle Produkte aus einem Radius von 120 km stammen – dem Herd am nächsten liegen der hofeigene Gemüsegarten sowie der Moorsee, aus dem man den Fisch fürs Abendessen selbst herausangeln darf. Der See zählt überhaupt zu den schönsten Accessoires des Hauses, vor allem im Sommer, wenn das Wasser bis zu 26 Grad warm wird. ◆ Buchtipp: „Die Ursache" von Thomas Bernhard.

ANREISE *Idyllisch am Goldegger See im Pongau gelegen, 60 km vom Flughafen Salzburg entfernt* · **PREIS** *€€–€€€* · **ZIMMER** *22 Zimmer und 5 Suiten* · **KÜCHE** *Die kreative regionale Küche wird regelmäßig vom Gault&Millau ausgezeichnet* · **GESCHICHTE** *Die ältesten Mauern des Seehofs stammen von 1727. Susi und Sepp Schellhorn führen den Familienbetrieb in fünfter Generation* · **X-FAKTOR** *Die regelmäßigen Lesungen, oft mit Schauspielern vom Burgtheater*

L'ART AU BORD DU LAC

Même les rédacteurs en chef critiques et les écrivains exigeants sont en extase au Seehof : l'un d'eux évoquait un « établissement envoûtant » ; « celui qui ne vit pas ici ne sait pas ce qu'est la vie », jugeait un deuxième, et un troisième résumait « au Seehof, je suis plus à la maison que chez moi ». Avec un grand sens de la culture, de l'art et de la gastronomie, Susi et Sepp Schellhorn ont créé un lieu tout à fait particulier, qu'ils considèrent plus comme une maison destinée à des amis que comme un hôtel. Chez eux, il faut décélérer, se détendre dans les pièces thématiques conçues par des artistes et des designers, trouver sa nouvelle littérature préférée dans la bibliothèque qui abrite toutes les premières éditions de la maison d'édition Suhrkamp, et se laisser inspirer par les peintures originales modernes partout dans la maison (la collection qui comprend, entre autres, des trésors de Gerhard Richter et Maria Lassnig, est déjà plus vaste que les surfaces murales disponibles). Dans la cuisine ouverte du Restaurant Hecht r120, on peut regarder le chef réinterpréter les recettes de l'ancien livre de cuisine familial. L'ajout « r120 » signifie que presque tout est produit dans un rayon de 120 km – les denrées les plus proches du fourneau se trouvent dans le potager de la ferme et le lac où vous pouvez pêcher votre propre poisson pour le dîner. Le lac est l'un des plus beaux atouts de la maison, surtout en été quand la température de l'eau monte à 26 degrés. ◆ À lire : « L'Origine » de Thomas Bernhard.

ACCÈS *Situé de manière idyllique au bord du lac de Goldegg à Pongau, à 60 km de l'aéroport de Salzbourg* · **PRIX** *€€–€€€* · **CHAMBRES** *22 chambres et 5 suites* · **RESTAURATION** *Cuisine régionale innovante régulièrement récompensée par le Gault&Millau* · **HISTOIRE** *Les murs les plus anciens du Seehof datent de 1727. Susi et Sepp Schellhorn dirigent l'entreprise familiale dont ils représentent la cinquième génération* · **LES « PLUS »** *Les lectures organisées régulièrement ; souvent avec des comédiens du Burgtheater*

MEZI PLŮTKY

ČELADNÁ, CARPATHIAN MOUNTAINS
CZECH REPUBLIC

MEZI PLŮTKY

Čeladná 266, Czech Republic
Tel. + 420 606 92 42 32 · meziplutky@gmail.com
www.meziplutky.cz

BETWEEN THE FENCES

The Beskids, a mountain range in the western Carpathians, are one of the least-known and most untouched upland regions in Europe. Much of the woodland has the character of primeval forest, with protected flora and fauna. Here the architect Daniela Hradilova and the antique collector and gardener Petr Hradil discovered a 200-year-old farmhouse, which they restored, in their own words, "on tiptoe", with care, modesty and respect for its history. They retained the shingle roof, the heavy ceiling beams and small windows, but at the same time introduced a surprising amount of light and spaciousness to the interior thanks to tall glass doors, light-colored sandstone floors and whitewashed walls. Simple items of furniture made from honey-colored wood are juxtaposed with designer chairs by Karl Andersson & Söner, Hay, Ronan Bouroullec and Patricia Urquiola, while in the room named The Daughter, the woolly white rocking-sheep by Povl Kjer stands guard by the bed (by the way, it is the only sheep that you need to count, as the wonderful tranquillity of the house means you fall asleep in record time). The other rooms, named The Parents, The Son and The Guest, accommodate two to four persons and have modern, open bathrooms. The kitchen, the dining room with an open fire, the conservatory and the garden with its natural pond are shared by guests. The site is surrounded by the typical wooden fences that gave the house its name: Mezi Plůtky means "between the fences". ◆ Book to pack: "The Unbearable Lightness of Being" by Milan Kundera.

DIRECTIONS *In a pretty valley near Čeladná, 39 km/24 miles south of Ostrava* · **RATES** *€€* · **ROOMS** *4 rooms. Children from the age of 12 upwards only (except when the whole house is booked exclusively)* · **FOOD** *Home-made cake and jam, as well as fresh ingredients from the nearby area, are served at breakfast; in the evening, guests can either order a meal to be cooked or cook themselves* · **HISTORY** *Opened in 2017 as a boutique hotel* · **X-FACTOR** *The wonderful view of the natural surroundings*

ZWISCHEN DEN ZÄUNEN

Die Beskiden, ein Gebirgszug der Westkarpaten, sind eine der unbekanntesten und unberührtesten Bergregionen Europas – viele ihrer Wälder haben noch Urwaldcharakter mit einer naturgeschützten Flora und Fauna. Hier entdeckten die Architektin Daniela Hradilova und der Antiquitätensammler und Gärtner Petr Hradil ein 200 Jahre altes Bauernhaus, das sie nach eigenen Worten „auf Zehenspitzen" mit Sorgfalt, Zurückhaltung sowie Respekt für seine Geschichte renovierten. So behielten sie das Schindeldach, die mächtigen Deckenbalken und kleinen Fenster bei, verliehen aber zugleich dem Inneren des Gebäudes mit hohen Glastüren, hellen Sandsteinböden und weiß getünchten Wänden überraschend viel Licht und Weite. Schlichte Möbel aus honigfarbenem Holz stehen neben Designerstühlen von Karl Andersson & Söner, Hay, Ronan Bouroullec oder Patricia Urquiola, und im Zimmer „Die Tochter" wacht das wollweiße Schaukelschaf von Povl Kjer neben dem Bett (es ist im Übrigen das einzige Schaf, das man zählen muss, denn dank der wundervollen Ruhe schläft man in Rekordzeit ein). „Die Eltern", „Der Sohn" und „Der Gast" heißen die weiteren Räume, die zwei bis vier Besuchern Platz bieten und moderne, offene Bäder besitzen. Die Küche, das Esszimmer mit Kamin, den Wintergarten und den Garten mit Naturteich teilen sich die Besucher. Umgeben wird das Grundstück von typischen Holzzäunen, die dem Haus seinen Namen gaben: Mezi Plůtky bedeutet „zwischen den Zäunen". ◆ Buchtipp: „Die unerträgliche Leichtigkeit des Seins" von Milan Kundera.

ANREISE *In einem malerischen Tal nahe der Gemeinde Čeladná gelegen, 39 km südlich von Ostrava* · PREIS €€ · ZIMMER *4 Zimmer. Kinder werden erst ab 12 Jahren empfangen (außer bei Exklusivbuchung des ganzen Hauses)* · KÜCHE *Zum Frühstück gibt es selbst gemachte Kuchen und Marmelade sowie Frisches aus der Umgebung; abends kann man sich bekochen lassen oder selbst am Herd stehen* · GESCHICHTE *2017 als Boutiquehotel eröffnet* · X-FAKTOR *Der herrliche Blick auf die umliegende Natur*

ENTRE LES CLÔTURES

Les Beskides, une chaîne de montagnes des Carpates occidentales, sont l'une des régions montagneuses les plus méconnues et les mieux préservées d'Europe – beaucoup de leurs forêts ont conservé leur caractère de forêt primaire et abritent une flore et une faune protégées. L'architecte Daniela Hradilova et le collectionneur d'antiquités et jardinier Petr Hradil y ont découvert une ferme bicentenaire qu'ils ont, selon leurs propres termes, restaurée « sur la pointe des pieds » avec soin, modestie et respect pour son histoire. Ils ont ainsi conservé le toit de bardeaux, les imposantes poutres de plafond et les petites fenêtres ; en même temps ils ont donné une quantité surprenante de lumière et d'espace à l'intérieur du bâtiment en le dotant de hautes portes vitrées, de sols en grès brillant et de murs blanchis à la chaux. Des meubles aux lignes sobres en bois couleur miel côtoient les chaises design de Karl Andersson & Söner, Hay, Ronan Bouroullec ou Patricia Urquiola, et dans la chambre « La Fille », le mouton à bascule en laine blanche de Povl Kjer veille à côté du lit (c'est le seul mouton que vous devrez compter, le calme est tel que l'on s'endort en un temps record). « Les Parents », « Le Fils » et « L'Hôte » sont les noms des autres chambres, qui peuvent abriter deux à quatre personnes et disposent de salles de bains modernes et ouvertes. Les visiteurs se partagent la cuisine, la salle à manger équipée d'une cheminée, le jardin d'hiver et le jardin avec étang naturel. La propriété est entourée de clôtures en bois typiques, d'où le nom de la maison : Mezi Plůtky signifie « entre les clôtures ». ◆ À lire : « L'Insupportable Légèreté de l'être » de Milan Kundera.

ACCÈS *Dans une vallée pittoresque à proximité de la commune de Čeladná, à 39 km au sud d'Ostrava* · PRIX €€ · CHAMBRES *4 chambres. Les enfants ne sont accueillis qu'à partir de 12 ans (à moins que la maison n'ait été entièrement louée)* · RESTAURATION *Gâteaux et confitures faits maison au petit déjeuner, ainsi que des produits frais des alentours ; le soir on peut se laisser régaler ou cuisiner soi-même* · HISTOIRE *La maison a ouvert ses portes en 2017 comme boutique-hôtel* · LES « PLUS » *La vue sublime sur la nature environnante*

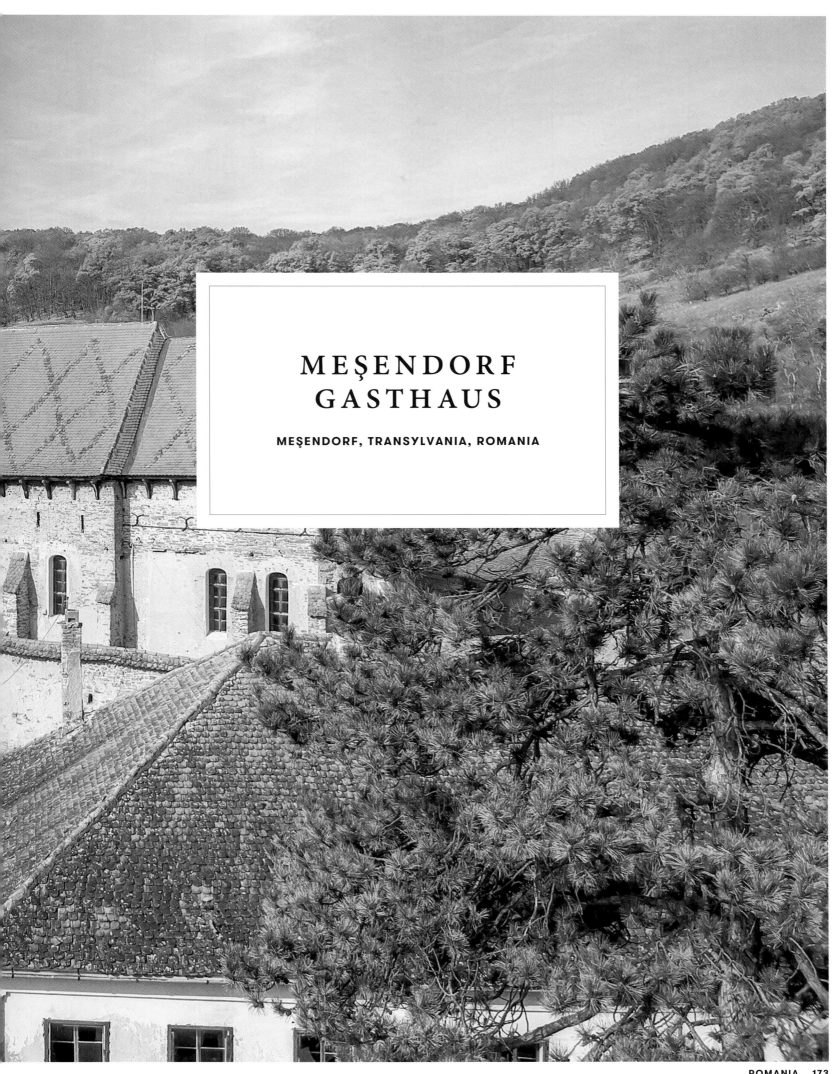

MEȘENDORF
GASTHAUS

MEȘENDORF, TRANSYLVANIA, ROMANIA

MEŞENDORF GASTHAUS

Strada Principala 48-49, Meşendorf, Romania
Tel. + 40 799 782 398 · contact@mesendorfgasthaus.ro
www.mesendorfgasthaus.ro

THE SAXON HERITAGE OF SIEBENBÜRGEN

Transylvania, the mysterious country "beyond the woods", is known to many people only as the fictional home of the world's most famous vampire: the infamous Prince Vlad, who put his enemies on stakes and is said to have drunk their blood, lived here. He was the model for Bram Stoker's legendary Count Dracula. But his region at the heart of Romania has much more to offer than horror stories. It is one of the most pristine areas of Europe – with extensive wildflower meadows, ancient oak and beech forests, the habitat of endangered animal species, and seven defensive castles that Saxon settlers built in the 12th and 13th centuries, giving the province the German name Siebenbürgen, meaning "seven castles". Meşendorf Gasthaus keeps firmly to the style of the Siebenbürgen Saxons. Historic farm buildings and newly constructed additions built according to traditional artisan methods form a group around an idyllic courtyard, and are equipped with wooden ceilings and floors, simple rustic furniture and country accessories. A true gem is the barn, more than 100 years old, which today houses the dining room and a gallery from which guests can admire from close up the original structure of roof beams. Around the estate lie an enchanting garden and authentic villages such as Meşendorf and Viscri, where there is a reasonable chance of running into a high-born person who is harmless in comparison to Count Dracula: Prince Charles is a great fan of this area, not only a regular guest but also a landowner here. He bought several farmers' houses and restored them in cooperation with a local foundation to preserve this heritage. ◆ Book to pack: "Wasted Morning" by Gabriela Adamesteanu.

DIRECTIONS *90 km/55 miles north-west of Braşov. The nearest international airport is Bucharest (about 250 km/155 miles)* · **RATES** € · **ROOMS** *7 rooms (4 in the main building, 3 in the annex), one of which even has a private sauna* · **FOOD** *Breakfast is served, and on request lunch or dinner on the basis of traditional local recipes* · **HISTORY** *The main building dates from 1919. Since April 2018 the farm has been a guest house* · **X-FACTOR** *A wonderful combination of old and new – in natural surroundings*

DAS ERBE DER SIEBENBÜRGER SACHSEN

Transsilvanien, das geheimnisvolle „Land hinter den Wäldern", ist vielen nur als imaginäre Heimat des berühmtesten Vampirs der Welt bekannt: Hier lebte einst der berüchtigte Fürst Vlad, der seine Feinde aufgespießt und ihr Blut getrunken haben soll – er war Vorbild für Bram Stokers legendären „Graf Dracula". Doch die Region im Herzen Rumäniens hat viel mehr zu bieten als Gruselgeschichten. Sie ist eines der ursprünglichsten Gebiete Europas – mit weiten Wildblumenwiesen, uralten Eichen- und Buchenwäldern, in denen vom Aussterben bedrohte Tierarten leben, sowie sieben Wehrburgen, die deutsche Siedler im 12. und 13. Jahrhundert erbauten und die ihr zum Namen Siebenbürgen verhalfen. Ganz im Stil der Siebenbürger Sachsen ist auch das Meşendorf Gasthaus gehalten. Historische Hofgebäude und nach traditioneller Handwerkskunst neu errichtete Anbauten gruppieren sich um einen idyllischen Innenhof und sind mit Holzdecken und -böden, schlichten Bauernmöbeln sowie rustikalen Accessoires ausgestattet. Ein Schmuckstück ist der mehr als 100 Jahre alte Stadel, der heute den Speisesaal umfasst sowie eine Galerie, von der man die originale Dachbalkenkonstruktion aus nächster Nähe bestaunen kann. Rund um das Anwesen liegen ein verwunschener Garten und authentische Dörfer wie Meşendorf oder Viscri, wo gute Chancen bestehen, einem im Vergleich zu Graf Dracula harmlosen Adligen über den Weg zu laufen: Prinz Charles ist ein großer Fan der Gegend und nicht nur regelmäßiger Gast, sondern auch Grundbesitzer: Er erwarb hier mehrere Bauernhäuser und sanierte sie gemeinsam mit einer örtlichen Stiftung, um sie zu erhalten. ◆ Buchtipp: „Der verlorene Morgen" von Gabriela Adameşteanu.

ANREISE *90 km nordwestlich von Braşov gelegen. Nächster internationaler Flughafen ist Bukarest (rund 250 km)* · **PREIS** *€* · **ZIMMER** *7 Zimmer (4 im Haupthaus, 3 im Anbau), eines sogar mit privater Sauna* · **KÜCHE** *Außer Frühstück bekommt man auf Anfrage auch Mittag- und Abendessen. Gekocht wird nach überlieferten lokalen Rezepten* · **GESCHICHTE** *Das historische Haupthaus stammt von 1919. Seit April 2018 ist der Hof ein Gasthaus* · **X-FAKTOR** *Eine wunderbare Kombination aus Alt und Neu – mitten in der Natur*

L'HÉRITAGE DES SAXONS DE TRANSYLVANIE

La plupart d'entre nous ne connaissent la Transylvanie, le mystérieux pays « au-delà des forêts », que parce qu'elle évoque le vampire le plus célèbre du monde : c'est ici qu'a vécu le tristement célèbre prince Vlad, empalant ses ennemis et buvant leur sang – il a servi de modèle au légendaire « Dracula » de Bram Stoker. Mais cette région située au cœur de la Roumanie a beaucoup plus à offrir que des histoires effrayantes. C'est l'une des régions d'Europe ayant le mieux gardé leur état d'origine – avec ses vastes prairies émaillées de fleurs sauvages, ses forêts de chênes et de hêtres séculaires où vivent des espèces menacées, et ses sept châteaux fortifiés construits par les colons allemands aux XIIe et XIIIe siècles (d'où son nom allemand « Siebenbürgen »). L'hôtel Meşendorf est également dans le style des Saxons de Transylvanie. Les bâtiments historiques de la ferme et les annexes récemment construites dans les règles de l'artisanat traditionnel sont regroupés autour d'une cour intérieure idyllique et abritent des plafonds et planchers en bois, du mobilier paysan simple et des accessoires rustiques. La grange plus que centenaire, qui abrite aujourd'hui la salle à manger ainsi qu'une galerie d'où l'on peut admirer de près la construction originale des poutres du toit est un véritable bijou. La propriété est entourée d'un jardin enchanteur et de villages authentiques comme Meşendorf ou Viscri, où les chances ne sont pas minces de rencontrer un aristocrate tout à fait inoffensif celui-là. Le Prince Charles, grand admirateur de la région, vient régulièrement, mais il est aussi un propriétaire terrien : il a acheté plusieurs fermes et les a rénovées avec une fondation locale pour préserver leur patrimoine. ◆ À lire : « Une matinée perdue » de Gabriela Adameşteanu.

ACCÈS *À 90 km au nord-ouest de Braşov. L'aéroport international le plus proche est à Bucarest (environ 250 km)* · **PRIX** *€* · **CHAMBRES** *7 chambres (4 dans la maison principale, 3 dans l'annexe), l'une dispose même d'un sauna privé* · **RESTAURATION** *Petit déjeuner inclus, déjeuner et dîner sur demande. Les plats sont préparés d'après des recettes locales traditionnelles* · **HISTOIRE** *La maison principale historique date de 1919. La ferme est un hôtel depuis avril 2018* · **LES « PLUS »** *Une combinaison merveilleuse d'ancien et de nouveau – en pleine nature*

ROOMS HOTELS

KAZBEGI & TBILISI, GEORGIA

ROOMS HOTELS

1 V. Gorgalasi Street, Kazbegi, Georgia
Tel. + 995 322 400 099 · kazbegi@roomshotels.com

14 Merab Kostava Street, Tbilisi, Georgia
Tel. + 995 322 020 099 · tbilisi@roomshotels.com
www.roomshotels.com

A GUEST IN GEORGIA

"A guest is sent by God", says a Georgian proverb – so it is hardly surprising that the locals do all they can to prepare a heavenly welcome for their visitors. They receive travellers with both warmth and pride, tell them the turbulent history of Georgia, spoil them with the delights of their still little-known cuisine and reveal their own personal favorite places. To find particularly good hosts, talk to the staff of the Rooms Hotels – a young, independent company that takes inspiration from its local roots as well as from international trends. With boldness, entrepreneurial spirit and a sure sense of style, Rooms Hotels opened its first house in Kazbegi in the Caucasus, transforming a former sanatorium into a modern lodge. From the rustic, minimalistic rooms, from the indoor pool and from the outdoor veranda there is a spectacular view of the mountains, which are wonderful terrain for walking and skiing. After a few days in natural surroundings, if you long for city life again you can book a room in the sister hotel in Tbilisi, which is housed in a decommissioned printworks. A local architects' office, Adjara Arch, renovated the complex in industrial style with glass, iron and wood, and fitted it with printed wallpaper, dark leather furniture and vintage accessories. The rooms on the top floor are specially recommended. From their terraces, guests can look up across the roofs and wave gratefully to God. ◆ Book to pack: "The Eighth Life" by Nino Haratischvili.

DIRECTIONS *Rooms Hotel Tbilisi is situated in Vera, the artists' quarter. Kazbegi is best reached by car (150 km/95 miles north of Tbilisi)* · RATES *€–€€* · ROOMS *155 rooms in Kazbegi, 125 in Tbilisi* · FOOD *Typical Georgian dishes, creatively refined* · HISTORY *Rooms Hotel Kazbegi opened in 2012, the hotel in Tbilisi followed in 2014* · X-FACTOR *The hotels arrange first-class guides for mountain and city tours*

ZU GAST IN GEORGIEN

„Ein Gast ist von Gott gesandt", sagt ein georgisches Sprichwort – kein Wunder also, dass die Einheimischen alles daran setzen, ihren Besuchern einen himmlischen Empfang zu bereiten. Mit ebenso viel Herz wie Stolz heißen sie Fremde willkommen, erzählen ihnen von der bewegten Geschichte Georgiens, verwöhnen sie mit den Köstlichkeiten einer noch recht unbekannten Küche und verraten ihnen ihre ganz persönlichen Lieblingsplätze. Besonders gute Gastgeber sind die Mitarbeiter der Rooms Hotels – einem jungen und unabhängigen Unternehmen, das sich von seinen lokalen Wurzeln ebenso inspirieren lässt wie von internationalen Trends. Mit Mut, Unternehmergeist und Stilsicherheit eröffneten die Rooms Hotels ihr erstes Haus in Kazbegi im Kaukasus, wo sie ein ehemaliges Sanatorium in eine moderne Lodge verwandelten. Aus den rustikal-minimalistischen Zimmern, vom Innenpool und von der Außenveranda eröffnet sich eine spektakuläre Sicht auf die Berge, die ein wunderbares Wander- und Skirevier sind. Wer sich nach ein paar Tagen in der Natur wieder nach Stadtleben sehnt, kann ein Zimmer im Schwesterhotel in Tiflis reservieren, das in einer stillgelegten Druckerei entstand. Das örtliche Architekturbüro Adjara Arch hat den Komplex mit Glas, Eisen sowie Holz im Industriestil renoviert und mit bedruckten Tapeten, dunklen Ledermöbeln und Vintageaccessoires ausgestattet. Besonders empfehlenswert sind die Zimmer in der obersten Etage, von deren Terrassen man über die Dächer nach oben blicken und Gott zum Dank zuwinken kann. ◆ Buchtipp: „Das achte Leben" von Nino Haratischwili.

ANREISE *Das Rooms Hotel Tiflis liegt im Künstlerviertel Vera. Kazbegi ist am besten mit dem Auto zu erreichen (150 km nördlich von Tiflis)* · PREIS *€–€€* · ZIMMER *155 Zimmer in Kazbegi, 125 in Tiflis* · KÜCHE *Typische georgische Gerichte, kreativ verfeinert* · GESCHICHTE *Das Rooms Hotel Kazbegi eröffnete 2012, das Haus in Tiflis folgte 2014* · X-FAKTOR *Die Hotels vermitteln erstklassige Guides für Berg- und Stadttouren*

INVITÉ EN GÉORGIE

« L'hôte est un envoyé de Dieu », dit un proverbe géorgien – rien d'étonnant donc si les gens du pays font tout ce qu'ils peuvent pour recevoir divinement leurs visiteurs. Avec autant de générosité que de fierté, ils accueillent les étrangers, leur racontent l'histoire mouvementée de la Géorgie, les entourent d'attentions en leur faisant goûter les délices d'une cuisine encore méconnue, et leur révèlent leurs lieux de prédilection personnels. Les employés des Rooms Hotels – une entreprise jeune et indépendante, inspirée par ses racines locales autant que par les tendances internationales – sont des hôtes particulièrement prévenants. Avec courage, esprit d'entreprise et style, les Rooms Hotels ont ouvert leur premier hôtel à Kazbegui (Stepantsminda), dans le Caucase, transformant un ancien sanatorium en un pavillon moderne. Les chambres rustiques et minimalistes, la piscine intérieure et la véranda extérieure offrent des vues spectaculaires sur les montagnes, qui sont un magnifique domaine de randonnée et de ski. Ceux qui, après quelques jours dans la nature, rêvent à nouveau de la vie en ville peuvent réserver une chambre à Tbilissi, dans un hôtel construit dans une imprimerie désaffectée. Le bureau d'architecture local Adjara Arch a rénové le complexe avec du verre, du fer et du bois dans un style industriel et l'a agrémenté de papier peint imprimé, de meubles en cuir foncé et d'accessoires vintage. Les chambres du dernier étage sont particulièrement recommandées. De leurs terrasses, on peut voir au-dessus des toits et faire un signe de la main au Père céleste pour le remercier. ◆ À lire : « La Huitième Vie » par Nino Haratischwili.

ACCÈS *Le Rooms Hotel Tbilisi est situé dans le quartier artistique de Vera. Kazbegui est accessible le plus facilement en voiture (à 150 km au nord de Tbilissi)* · PRIX *€–€€* · CHAMBRES *155 chambres à Kazbegui, 125 à Tbilissi* · RESTAURATION *Cuisine géorgienne typique, raffinée avec une belle inventivité* · HISTOIRE *Le Rooms Hotel de Kazbegui a ouvert ses portes en 2012, la maison de Tbilissi a suivi en 2014* · LES « PLUS » *Les hôtels communiquent les coordonnées de guides hors pair pour visiter la montagne et la ville*

AMMOS

CHANIA, CRETE, GREECE

AMMOS

Irakli Avgoula St., 73100 Chania, Crete, Greece
Tel. +30 28210 330 03 and +30 28210 330 25 · Tel. in winter: +30 6946 009686
info@ammoshotel.com · www.ammoshotel.com
Open from early April to late October

A SUMMER HOUSE

Thanks to its picturesque Venetian harbor guarded by an Egyptian lighthouse, its picture-postcard promenade with cafés and restaurants and the winding alleys of the Old Town lined by boutiques selling craft products, Chania is regarded as the most beautiful town in Crete, if not in the whole of Greece. Every bit as photogenic as the historic town center but in a wholly modern style, Hotel Ammos stands right by the beach and owes its name to its wonderful location: the Greek word "ammos" means "sand". Whereas it has a plain exterior in the white and sky-blue typical of the island, the hotel is a blaze of color inside. In collaboration with the architect Elisa Manola, the owner Nikos Tsepetis has fitted out the rooms so playfully and joyfully that guests immediately get a boost of good humor and energy when they enter. The designer chairs for the lobby, lounge and restaurant have been assembled with a passion for collecting and a sense of style – no one piece of furniture looks like another, and new items are added every year. The guest rooms have no television, but wonderful terrazzo floors,

beds by the Greek ecological brand Coco-Mat and chic extras such as colorful stools by Moroso, curtains by Kvadrat and original paintings by the Greek artist Konstantin Kakanias. Kitchenettes are also a standard feature – but are not really necessary, as the food, from the sumptuous breakfast for late risers to the exquisite dessert after dinner, is first-class and just as laid-back as the rest of the hotel. ◆ Book to pack: "Zorba the Greek" by Nikos Kazantzakis (there is a copy in every room).

DIRECTIONS *5 km/3 miles from the Old Town of Chania, 20 km/ 13 miles from Chania airport, 140 km/87 miles from Heraklion airport ·* **RATES** *€–€€€ ·* **ROOMS** *33 rooms with a garden or sea view. Several are rather small, and it is worth booking a room with a balcony or terrace ·* **FOOD** *Breakfast is served until 11:30 am. For lunch and dinner, classic Greek dishes get a modern interpretation – best enjoyed on the veranda ·* **HISTORY** *The hotel was opened in 1996 and redesigned from 2005 to 2008 ·* **X-FACTOR** *The exceptionally (family) friendly, personal service*

EIN SOMMERHAUS

Dank des malerischen venezianischen Hafens, über den ein ägyptischer Leuchtturm wacht, der Postkarten-Promenade mit Cafés und Restaurants sowie der verwinkelten Altstadtgassen, in denen sich Läden mit Kunsthandwerk Tür an Tür reihen, gilt Chania als schönste Stadt Kretas, wenn nicht sogar Griechenlands. Ebenso fotogen wie das historische Zentrum, aber in ganz modernem Stil zeigt sich das Hotel Ammos, das direkt am Strand steht und dieser herrlichen Lage seinen Namen verdankt – das griechische Wort „ammos" bedeutet „Sand". Außen schlicht im inseltypischen Weiß und Himmelblau gehalten, ist das Haus innen ein Farbenspiel. Gemeinsam mit der Architektin Elisa Manola hat der Besitzer Nikos Tsepetis die Räume so fröhlich und spielerisch ausgestattet, dass man beim Eintreten sofort gute Laune und neue Energie bekommt. Mit Sammlerleidenschaft und Stil wurden die Designerstühle für Lobby, Lounge und Restaurant zusammengetragen – kein Möbelstück gleicht dem anderen, und jedes Jahr kommen neue Modelle hinzu. In den Gästezimmern gibt es keine Fernseher, doch dafür wunderschöne Terrazzoböden, Betten der griechischen Öko-Marke Coco-Mat und schicke Extras wie bunte Hocker von Moroso, Vorhänge von Kvadrat und Originalbilder des griechischen Künstlers Konstantin Kakanias. Auch eine Kitchenette gehört zum Standard – wäre aber eigentlich nicht nötig, denn die Küche des Ammos ist vom üppigen Langschläferfrühstück bis zum feinen Dessert nach dem Dinner erstklassig und genauso entspannt wie der Rest des Hotels. ◆ Buchtipp: „Alexis Sorbas" von Nikos Kazantzakis (liegt in jedem Zimmer bereit).

ANREISE *5 km von Chanias Altstadt entfernt. Vom Flughafen Chania fährt man 20 km, vom Flughafen Heraklion 140 km ·* **PREIS** *€–€€€ ·* **ZIMMER** *33 Zimmer mit Garten- oder Meerblick. Einige sind recht klein, es lohnt sich, ein Zimmer mit Balkon oder Terrasse zu buchen ·* **KÜCHE** *Frühstück wird bis 11.30 Uhr serviert. Mittags und abends genießt man griechische Klassiker modern interpretiert – am schönsten auf der Veranda ·* **GESCHICHTE** *Das Hotel wurde 1996 eröffnet und von 2005 bis 2008 umgestaltet ·* **X-FAKTOR** *Der außergewöhnlich (familien-)freundliche, persönliche Service*

UN PAVILLON D'ÉTÉ

Son pittoresque port vénitien surveillé par un phare égyptien, sa promenade de carte postale avec cafés et restaurants et le labyrinthe de ruelles de la vieille ville, où les boutiques artisanales se suivent, font de La Canée la plus belle ville de Crète, sinon de Grèce. Tout aussi photogénique que le centre historique, mais dans un style très moderne, l'hôtel Ammos s'élève directement sur la plage et doit son nom à cet emplacement magnifique – en grec « ammos » signifie « sable ». L'extérieur est sobrement blanc et bleu ciel, ce qui est caractéristique de l'île, tandis que les espaces intérieurs jouent avec les couleurs. Avec l'architecte Elisa Manola, le propriétaire Nikos Tsepetis a aménagé les chambres de manière si joyeuse et ludique qu'elles dispensent immédiatement de la bonne humeur et un regain d'énergie. Les chaises design qui se trouvent dans le hall d'entrée, le salon et le restaurant ont été assemblées par un collectionneur passionné amoureux de l'élégance – aucun meuble ne ressemble à l'autre, et chaque année voit de nouveaux modèles arriver. Pas de télévision dans les chambres, mais de magnifiques sols en terrazzo, des lits de la marque grecque écologique Coco-Mat, des extras chic tels les tabourets colorés de Moroso et des rideaux de Kvadrat ainsi que des originaux de l'artiste grec Konstantin Kakanias. Elles possèdent toutes une kitchenette, ce qui ne serait pas nécessaire, car la cuisine de l'Ammos, de l'opulent petit déjeuner des amateurs de grasse matinée au dessert raffiné proposé après dîner, est aussi remarquable et décontractée que le reste de l'hôtel. ◆ À lire : « Alexis Zorba » de Nikos Kazantzakis (on le trouve dans toutes les chambres).

ACCÈS *À 5 km de la ville historique de La Canée. À 20 km de l'aéroport de La Canée, à 149 km de celui d'Héraklion ·* **PRIX** *€–€€€ ·* **CHAMBRES** *33 chambres avec vue sur le jardin ou la mer. Certaines sont très petites, réserver une chambre avec balcon ou terrasse en vaut la peine ·* **RESTAURATION** *Le petit déjeuner est servi jusqu'à 11h30. On peut savourer le midi et le soir des plats classiques grecs interprétés de manière moderne – la véranda est l'endroit idéal ·* **HISTOIRE** *L'hôtel a ouvert ses portes en 1996, son design a été repensé de 2005 à 2008 ·* **LES « PLUS »** *Le service exceptionnellement aimable (les enfants sont bienvenus) et soucieux du bien-être de chacun*

CHÂTEAU
DE BAGNOLS

BAGNOLS, AUVERGNE-RHÔNE-ALPES, FRANCE

CHÂTEAU DE BAGNOLS

69620 Bagnols, France
Tel: + 33 474 714 000 · info@chateaudebagnols.fr
www.chateaudebagnols.com

MAJESTIC SECLUSION

Lord of all you can see – at least this could be your dream, as you look out from the ramparts of what was once a fortress, and now is a secluded retreat. Complete with moat and drawbridge, the Château de Bagnols stands on a high vantage point in the lovely Burgundy countryside, guarding its guests from the public gaze and cares of the outside world. Hidden behind massive stone buttresses and towers are a fabulous hotel and garden, a haven for the fortunate few. First built in 1221 as a medieval stronghold, the Chateau is now one of France's historic monuments, restored to its rightful splendor. Its portcullis opens to reveal peaceful gardens and terraces, sheltered by yew hedges and encircled by a stone wall. After entering the castle's courtyard, the arriving guests step into an atmosphere of history and grandeur. Many of the rooms have striking Renaissance wall paintings, uncovered during recent restoration. Antique beds are hung with period silk velvets and embroideries; rich tapestries adorn walls, and great, elaborately carved fireplaces blaze out warmth in the winter. The famous vineyards of Beaujolais and the charming towns and villages in the rolling green hills and valleys beyond may well tempt you out from your castle realm. ◆ Book to pack: "The Red and the Black" by Stendhal.

DIRECTIONS *24 km/15 miles north of Lyon* · RATES *€€€€* · ROOMS *27 rooms, including suites* · FOOD *French gastronomic and French bistronomic menu* · HISTORY *Built in 1221, the château has been transformed several times over the centuries. The hotel was opened in 1991* · X-FACTOR *Regal rural retreat, privacy assured*

MAJESTÄTISCHE RUHE

Wenn man vom Schutzwall dieser ehemaligen Festung um sich schaut, fühlt man sich wie der Herr über die unten liegenden Ländereien. Denn das Château de Bagnols, umgeben von einem Graben mit einer Ziehbrücke, überragt majestätisch die liebliche Landschaft des Burgund. Heute birgt es ein abgeschiedenes Plätzchen, das Schutz vor der Außenwelt bietet. Versteckt hinter massiven steinernen Pfeilern und Türmen befindet sich ein Hotel mit einem wunderschönen Garten, in dem es sich herrlich entspannen lässt. Das im Jahr 1221 errichtete mittelalterliche Château gehört heute zu Frankreichs Baudenkmälern. Hinter seinem Falltor erstrecken sich friedliche Gärten und Terrassen, geschützt durch Eibenhecken und eine steinerne Mauer. Sobald man den Burghof betritt, verzaubert eine ganz besondere Atmosphäre die Besucher. Viele der Zimmer bestechen durch eindrucksvolle Wandgemälde aus der Renaissance, die erst vor Kurzem freigelegt wurden. Seidensamtvorhänge und Stickereien zieren die antiken Betten; die Wände sind mit üppigen Gobelins behängt, und große Kamine mit kunstvollen Einfassungen verbreiten im Winter wohlige Wärme. Doch die berühmten Weinberge des Beaujolais sowie die reizenden Städte und Dörfer, die verstreut über die umgebenden Hügel und Täler liegen, sind geschaffen dafür, Sie auch gelegentlich hinter den Burgmauern hervorzulocken. ◆ Buchtipp: „Rot und Schwarz" von Stendhal.

ANREISE *24 km nördlich von Lyon* · PREIS *€€€€* · ZIMMER *27 Zimmer, einschließlich mehrerer Suiten* · KÜCHE *Französische Küche und Menüs* · GESCHICHTE *Das Gebäude wurde 1221 errichtet und über die Jahrhunderte mehrfach umgebaut. Als Hotel wurde es 1991 eröffnet* · X-FAKTOR *Königliches, ländliches Refugium mit garantiertem Schutz der Privatsphäre*

UNE RETRAITE MAJESTUEUSE

Montez sur les remparts de cet ancien château fort, aujourd'hui paisible retraite, et imaginez-vous seigneur des lieux qui s'étendent sous votre regard. Avec ses douves et son pont-levis, le château de Bagnols, érigé dans une situation admirable, domine la ravissante campagne bourguignonne. Derrière ses tours et contreforts massifs se cachent un hôtel fabuleux et un charmant parc, paradis pour les happy few. Forteresse médiévale dont la construction débute en 1221, ce château classé monument historique a retrouvé sa splendeur d'antan. La herse se lève pour révéler des jardins et terrasses paisibles, abrités derrière des haies d'ifs et entourés d'un mur en pierre. Histoire et splendeur accueillent les hôtes dès leur arrivée dans la cour du château. Un grand nombre des salles sont revêtues de magnifiques fresques Renaissance, découvertes durant la récente restauration. Les lits anciens sont fermés par des rideaux de velours de soie et de dentelles d'époque ; de riches tapisseries ornent les murs et, en hiver, les grandes cheminées sculptées avec art font rayonner leur chaleur. Les célèbres vignobles du Beaujolais ainsi que les jolis bourgs et villages qui émaillent ce paysage de collines et vallées verdoyantes vous inciteront certainement à quitter les murs de votre château de rêve. ◆ À lire : « Le Rouge et le Noir » de Stendhal.

ACCÈS *À 24 km au nord de Lyon* · PRIX *€€€€* · CHAMBRES *27 chambres dont des suites* · RESTAURATION *Gastronomie française et menu français bistronomique* · HISTOIRE *Construit en 1221, le bâtiment a été transformé plusieurs fois au cours des siècles. L'hôtel a ouvert en 1991* · LES « PLUS » *Retraite rurale royale, tranquillité garantie*

LES MAISONS MARINES D'HUCHET

VIELLE-SAINT-GIRONS, NOUVELLE-AQUITAINE, FRANCE

LES MAISONS MARINES D'HUCHET

40320 Eugénie-les-Bains, France
Tel: + 33 558 050 607 · reservation@michelguerard.com
www.michelguerard.com

FAR FROM THE MADDING CROWD

A tall structure often marks the site of somewhere special. In a distant place in France, far from the crowds that flock to see his famous Parisian tower, there is a small marine beacon built by Gustave Eiffel. It also marks a special spot. On the Atlantic coast between Bordeaux and Biarritz there are many miles of deserted beaches, edged by forests of pine trees. Hidden amongst the sand dunes is a tiny retreat where the motto is "keep it simple". Les Maisons Marines consist of just three beach houses, an unusual trio. The distinctive main house was built some 150 years ago as a hunting lodge. The other two houses, once boat sheds, are now charming little guest cottages set apart in this quiet hideaway. Access to Les Maisons Marines is circuitous: there is no direct route to here, because first you must stay at one of Michel and Christine Guérard's hotels at Eugénie-les-Bains, like Les Prés d'Eugénie, to gain admittance to the beach houses. They are more like a private home than a hotel, one the owners invite you to share, and a special place to take time out and savor the solitude. The sound of the surf will lull you to sleep. ◆ Book to pack: "Les Misérables" by Victor Hugo.

DIRECTIONS *150 km/93 miles south from Bordeaux airport* · **RATES** *€€€* · **ROOMS** *2 houses that accommodate two people* · **FOOD** *Menus by a master chef* · **HISTORY** *Built in the middle of the 19th century, Les Maisons Marines opened as guest houses in December 1999* · **X-FACTOR** *Solitude and scenery with special surroundings and food*

ABSEITS DES MASSENTOURISMUS

Es kommt häufig vor, dass ein Ort, der etwas Außergewöhnliches zu bieten hat, durch ein hohes Bauwerk gekennzeichnet ist. In einem entlegenen Winkel an der Westküste Frankreichs, weitab von den Touristenmassen, die sich um Gustave Eiffels berühmten Turm in Paris drängen, steht ein kleiner, vom selben Ingenieur erbauter Leuchtturm, der mit Sicherheit auf einen ganz besonderen Ort verweist. Zwischen Bordeaux und Biarritz erstrecken sich entlang der Atlantikküste lange, einsame Strände, die von Pinienwäldern geschützt werden. Versteckt in den Sanddünen liegt ein kleines Refugium, in dem das Motto „Weniger ist mehr" stilvoll gelebt wird. Les Maisons Marines sind genau drei Strandhäuser: Das markante Haupthaus wurde vor etwa 150 Jahren als Jagdhütte erbaut. Die beiden anderen Gebäude dienten früher als Bootshäuser und sind heute bezaubernde kleine Ferienhäuschen, die ganz im Verborgenen liegen. Es ist jedoch ein Umweg nötig, um nach Les Maisons Marines zu kommen, denn Sie müssen zuvor in einem der Hotels von Michel und Christine Guérard in Eugénie-les-Bains, wie etwa dem Les Prés d'Eugénie, zu Gast gewesen sein. In den Strandhäusern sind Sie dann eher privilegierter Hausgast der Besitzer als Hotelbesucher. Nutzen Sie die Abgeschiedenheit, um zur Ruhe zu kommen, und lassen Sie sich nachts vom Rauschen des Meeres in den Schlaf wiegen. ◆ Buchtipp: „Die Elenden" von Victor Hugo.

ANREISE *150 km südlich vom internationalen Flughafen Bordeaux ·* PREIS *€€€ ·* ZIMMER *2 Häuser für je 2 Personen ·* KÜCHE *Menüs von einem Spitzenkoch ·* GESCHICHTE *Les Maisons Marines wurden Mitte des 19. Jahrhunderts erbaut und werden seit Dezember 1999 als Gästehäuser genutzt ·* X-FAKTOR *Abgeschiedenheit, schöne Umgebung und hervorragendes Essen*

LOIN DES FOULES

Il est fréquent qu'un lieu extraordinaire se distingue par un bâtiment de haute taille. Dans un coin reculé de France, loin des foules qui affluent pour visiter la célèbre tour Eiffel à Paris, se trouve un petit phare également construit par Gustave Eiffel, soulignant lui aussi un lieu remarquable. De Bordeaux à Biarritz, la côte Atlantique s'étend sur des kilomètres de plages désertes, bordées de forêts de pins. Dans les dunes se cache une retraite minuscule où le mot d'ordre est « simplicité ». Au nombre de trois, ces Maisons Marines forment un trio original. La plus grande, d'aspect distinctif, est un ancien pavillon de chasse construit il y a environ 150 ans. Les deux autres, d'anciens hangars à bateaux, sont aujourd'hui de charmantes petites maisons d'hôtes, situées à l'écart dans cette retraite paisible. L'accès aux Maisons Marines se fait par des chemins détournés : pour y être admis, il faut d'abord séjourner dans l'un des hôtels de Michel et Christine Guérard, à Eugénie-les-Bains ou aux Prés d'Eugénie. Elles ressemblent moins à un hôtel qu'à des demeures privées que leur propriétaire vous aurait invité à partager. Dans ce lieu privilégié dont vous savourerez la solitude, vous vous reposerez, bercé par le clapotis des vagues. ◆ À lire : « Les Misérables » de Victor Hugo.

ACCÈS *À 150 km au sud de l'aéroport international de Bordeaux ·* PRIX *€€€ ·* CHAMBRES *2 maisons accueillant deux personnes ·* RESTAURATION *Cuisine d'un chef cuisinier ·* HISTOIRE *Construites au milieu du XIXᵉ siècle, les Maisons Marines ont ouvert leurs portes en décembre 1999 ·* LES « PLUS » *Solitude, cadre superbe et gastronomie*

LES PRÉS D'EUGÉNIE

EUGÉNIE-LES-BAINS, NOUVELLE-AQUITAINE, FRANCE

LES PRÉS D'EUGÉNIE

40320 Eugénie-les-Bains, France
Tel : + 33 558 050 607 · reservation@michelguerard.com
www.michelguerard.com

JOIE DE VIVRE

For some, this is a place of pilgrimage. Those who value fine dining come here to savor the great food and wine, devised by one of France's most well-known chefs. This is Michel Guérard's resort, where the ambience is as delicious as the food. Les Prés d'Eugénie are a cluster of hotels, restaurants, and a health spa. They have been described as being the model for what a country retreat should be. Indeed, this is the image of the good life. Guests are treated to a blend of herb gardens and climbing roses, exotic fragrances and delicious flavours, exquisite guest rooms, and sparkling springs. The mix of such fine ingredients makes this a very inviting setting. The old adage that two cooks are better than one does not apply here. Michel reigns over the cuisine, and his wife Christine has created the rest. The buildings, gardens, and the spa are her realm, while the restaurant is a national treasure, in a country that is famous for its food. The resort is in the village of Eugénie-les-Bains, in the heart of the Landes forest. It is a place so picturesque that it almost looks like a movie set. ◆ Book to pack: "How Proust Can Change Your Life" by Alain de Botton.

DIRECTIONS *Les Prés d'Eugénie are located in the village of Eugénie-les-Bains, in the heart of the Nouvelle-Aquitaine Region. Pau airport is 45 km/28 miles away, Bordeaux airport is 120 km/74 miles north* · RATES *€€€* · ROOMS *45 rooms and apartments* · FOOD *The raison d'être* · HISTORY *Les Prés d'Eugénie were built in the 18th century and opened in 1862 as hotel* · X-FACTOR *The art of living and eating*

JOIE DE VIVRE

Wer gute Küche zu schätzen weiß, der kommt hierher, um hervorragendes Essen und große Weine zu genießen. Sie werden kredenzt von Michel Guérard, einem der bekanntesten Köche des Landes, der hier seinen Wirkungsort hat. Das Ambiente des Hotels steht jedoch dem Essen in nichts nach. Les Prés d'Eugénie ist ein Ensemble aus mehreren Hotels, Restaurants und einer Wellnessanlage. Auf ideale Weise wird einem hier ein ruhiges Leben auf dem Land, ein Sinnbild für das Leben, wie es sein sollte, geboten. Der Gast wird verwöhnt mit duftenden Kräutergärten und rankenden Rosen, exotischen Düften und köstlichen Aromen, exquisiten Gästezimmern und perlenden Quellen. Die perfekte Mischung dieser Zutaten macht den Ort so einladend. Dass viele Köche den Brei verderben, nun, das weiß Michel Guérard. Deshalb hat er die Oberhoheit über die Küche, und seine Frau Christine kümmert sich um den Rest. Gebäude, Gärten und die Wellnessanlage sind ihr Reich, das Restaurant aber ist ein nationales Heiligtum. Die Hotelanlage liegt in dem malerischen Örtchen Eugénie-les-Bains im Herzen der Wälder der Landes. Hier ist es so pittoresk, dass man sich in einer Spielfilmkulisse zu befinden glaubt. ◆ Buchtipp: „Wie Proust Ihr Leben verändern kann" von Alain de Botton.

ANREISE *Im Dorf Eugénie-les-Bains im Herzen von Neu-Aquitanien gelegen. Der Flughafen von Pau ist 45 km entfernt, der Flughafen von Bordeaux liegt 120 km nördlich von Eugénie-les-Bains* · PREIS *€€€* · ZIMMER *45 Zimmer und Apartments* · KÜCHE *La raison d'être* · GESCHICHTE *Die Gebäude stammen aus dem 18. Jahrhundert. Das Hotel wurde 1862 eröffnet* · X-FAKTOR *Die Kunst zu leben und die Kunst zu essen*

JOIE DE VIVRE

Les amateurs de bonne chère viennent ici déguster d'excellents vins et une délicieuse cuisine concoctée par l'un des chefs les plus réputés de France. C'est le fief de Michel Guérard, et l'ambiance y est à la hauteur de la gastronomie. Les Prés d'Eugénie, qui regroupent plusieurs hôtels et restaurants ainsi qu'un centre thermal, ont été décrits comme un modèle de retraite champêtre. Pour beaucoup d'hôtes, il s'agit même d'un véritable lieu de pèlerinage. Il est vrai que le complexe est l'image même du « bien-être » : on y déambule parmi les plantes aromatiques et les roses grimpantes, les parfums exotiques et les odeurs alléchantes, les salons élégants et les sources d'eau chaude. Le mariage réussi de tous ces ingrédients forme un cadre résolument enchanteur. Michel Guérard règne sur la cuisine, dont l'éloge n'est plus à faire ; son épouse Christine s'occupe du reste : résidences, jardins et thermes. Le complexe hôtelier se trouve à Eugénie-les-Bains, au cœur de la forêt landaise ; une petite ville si pittoresque qu'on la croirait créée pour un film. ◆ À lire : « Comment Proust peut changer votre vie » d'Alain de Botton.

ACCÈS *Les Prés d'Eugénie sont situés à Eugénie-les-Bains, au centre de la Nouvelle-Aquitaine. L'aéroport de Pau se trouve à 45 km, celui de Bordeaux à 120 km au nord d'Eugénie-les-Bains* · PRIX *€€€* · CHAMBRES *45 chambres et appartements* · RESTAURATION *La raison d'être* · HISTOIRE *Construit au XVIIIe siècle, hôtel depuis 1862* · LES « PLUS » *L'art de vivre dans toute sa splendeur*

LA MIRANDE

AVIGNON, PROVENCE, FRANCE

LA MIRANDE

4, place de l'Amirande, 84000 Avignon, France
Tel: + 33 490 142 020 · mirande@la-mirande.fr
www.la-mirande.fr

INNER SANCTUM

In medieval times, Avignon was the residence of several popes. Conflicts within the Catholic Church as well as between the Pope and worldly powers were responsible for this relocation. The Pope's temporary displacement to Avignon resulted in a building fervor, as cardinals and prelates of the church strove to construct worthy earthly palaces and houses to dwell in. Originally the site of a 14th-century cardinal's residence, La Mirande is blessed with an ideal position. It is in the heart of the city, in a tranquil cobbled square, at the very foot of the Popes' Palace. Behind the hotel's original stone façade is an exquisite interior; one that bears testament to a real quest to attain a near faultless authenticity. Its success is such that even though it is relatively new, the interior seems to have evolved over generations and time. Meticulously restored, using the style and materials of the 17th and 18th century, La Mirande has all the splendor of an aristocratic residence of the era, together with the best of contemporary cuisine. Under the coffered ceiling of the restaurant, inventive fare that makes you truly grateful is served.
◆ Books to pack: "All Men are Mortal" by Simone de Beauvoir and "Tartarin de Tarascon" by Alphonse Daudet.

DIRECTIONS *1 hour's drive from Marseille airport; 2.5 hours south from Paris by TGV; in the center of Avignon* · RATES *€€€* · ROOMS *25 rooms and 1 suite* · FOOD *Two restaurants - one with French gourmet menus, one with rustic cuisine. There is also an in-house cookery school* · HISTORY *Originally built in the 14th century, La Mirande has been transformed several times. The hotel was opened in 1990* · X-FACTOR *Aristocratic interior and heavenly food*

IM ALLERHEILIGSTEN

Im Mittelalter war Avignon mehrfach für kurze Zeit Sitz des Papstes. Konflikte innerhalb der Kurie sowie zwischen Päpsten und weltlichen Mächten führten zu diesen unfreiwilligen Ortswechseln. Begleitet wurde der kurzzeitige Umzug nach Avignon von einem wahren Bauboom, denn Kardinäle und Prälaten der Kirche machten es sich zur Aufgabe, schon auf Erden Paläste und Häuser zu errichten, die ihrer würdig waren. Wo heute das Hotel La Mirande steht, befand sich im 14. Jahrhundert die Residenz eines Kardinals. Auch strategisch liegt das Hotel himmlisch, mitten im Herzen der Stadt nämlich, an einem verträumten Platz mit Kopfsteinpflaster, direkt am Fuß des Papstpalastes. Hinter der Originalfassade des Hotels versteckt sich ein herrliches Interieur, das auf Schritt und Tritt das Bestreben erkennen lässt, so viel Authentizität wie möglich herzustellen. Obwohl noch gar nicht alt, wirkt die Innengestaltung, als hätten an ihr ganze Generationen und Zeitläufte gewirkt. Im Stil des 17. und 18. Jahrhunderts bis ins Detail restauriert, strahlt La Mirande die Pracht einer aristokratischen Residenz aus und bietet gleichzeitig das Beste aus der heutigen Küche. Unter der Kassettendecke des Restaurants wird kreative Kochkunst geboten, die zu wahren Dankesgebeten verleitet. ◆ Buchtipps: „Alle Menschen sind sterblich" von Simone de Beauvoir und „Die Abenteuer des Herrn Tartarin aus Tarascon" von Alphonse Daudet.

ANREISE 1 Std. vom Flughafen Marseille entfernt; 2,5 Std. südlich von Paris mit dem TGV, im Zentrum von Avignon gelegen · PREIS €€€ · ZIMMER 25 Zimmer und 1 Suite · KÜCHE Zwei Restaurants – eines mit französischen Gourmetmenüs, eines mit rustikaler Küche. Zum Haus gehört auch eine Kochschule · GESCHICHTE Erbaut im 14. Jahrhundert, mehrfach über die Jahrhunderte umgebaut und 1990 als Hotel eröffnet · X-FAKTOR Aristokratisches Interieur und himmlisches Essen

INNER SANCTUM

Au Moyen Âge, Avignon fut pendant plusieurs courtes périodes la ville des Papes, lorsque des conflits au sein de la curie et entre la papauté et les pouvoirs temporels conduisirent à ce changement de résidence involontaire. L'installation du Pape en Avignon entraîna un boom dans la construction, les cardinaux et prélats rivalisant dans l'édification de palais et demeures luxueuses. Autrefois résidence d'un cardinal du XIVe siècle, l'hôtel La Mirande jouit d'une situation privilégiée. En plein cœur de la ville, sur une paisible place pavée, il se dresse au pied du Palais des Papes. Derrière la façade d'origine, se cache un ravissant intérieur qui se targue de rechercher une authenticité quasi parfaite. Cela avec grand succès, car bien qu'il soit relativement récent, l'intérieur de La Mirande semble avoir évolué au fil des générations et du temps. Méticuleusement restauré, dans le style et les matériaux des XVIIe et XVIIIe siècles, l'hôtel possède toute la splendeur d'une résidence aristocratique d'époque. S'y ajoute une cuisine contemporaine de grand chef ; sous le plafond à caissons du restaurant, de superbes plats originaux vous seront servis. ◆ À lire : « Tous les hommes sont mortels » de Simone de Beauvoir et « Aventures prodigieuses de Tartarin de Tarascon » d'Alphonse Daudet.

ACCÈS À 2 h 30 de Paris en TGV; à 1 h en voiture de l'aéroport de Marseille, en plein centre-ville d'Avignon · PRIX €€€ · CHAMBRES 25 chambres et 1 suite · RESTAURATION Un restaurant gastronomique et un restaurant offrant une cuisine du terroir. Cours de cuisine proposés · HISTOIRE Construit au XIVe siècle, le bâtiment a été transformé plusieurs fois au cours des siècles. L'hôtel a ouvert en 1990 · LES « PLUS » Intérieur aristocratique et cuisine succulente

L'ARLATAN

ARLES, PROVENCE, FRANCE

L'ARLATAN

20, rue du Sauvage, 13200 Arles, France
Tel. + 33 465 882 020 · contact@hotel-arlatan.fr
www.arlatan.com

A KALEIDOSCOPE

This site and building have a long and eventful history: in the time of the Roman Empire, a basilica stood here, and in the 15th century an urban residence in which the royal intendant Jean d'Arlatan received noble guests. Later downgraded to a military barracks, the house was converted in the late 1980s into an elegant hotel, which eventually passed into the ownership of Maja Hoffmann, a patron of the arts who loves Arles. She had the heritage-listed building thoroughly restored – under the direction of Jorge Pardo, an American artist with Cuban roots and a studio in Mexico. Known for his "all-round works of art", he made the Arlatan into something unique: both eccentric and eclectic, a hotel that combines the South American and southern French ways of life. On a wall and floor surface of 6,000 square meters he laid a mega-mosaic that is one of a kind, using almost two million tiles in eleven different shapes and 18 colors that were fired in a factory in Yucatan which had closed down but was reopened for this project. The retro-style furniture, made from sustainably grown guanacaste wood from Costa Rica, the imaginative lamps and the chandeliers are also his own designs – just like the paintings that decorate all doors and rooms, and were inspired by motifs in the work of Vincent van Gogh. On some of these paintings, Pardo has immortalised himself and the hotel owner too. It's fun to track them down… the journey of exploration can begin! ◆ Book to pack: "The Letters of Vincent van Gogh" by Johanna Gesina van Gogh-Bonger.

DIRECTIONS *In the historic center of Arles, 1 km/0.5 miles from the station (4 hours from Paris by high-speed train). The nearest airport is Marseille (70 km/45 miles)* · RATES *€–€€€* · ROOMS *35 rooms (in addition 6 rooms with a kitchen for "artists in residence" and 1 guest house)* · FOOD *The restaurant serves Provençal and Mediterranean dishes. There is also a chic cocktail bar* · HISTORY *The hotel opened in 2018 after a three-year renovation* · X-FACTOR *Designed down to the last detail: even the pool is adorned with a mosaic*

EIN KALEIDOSKOP

Dieses Grundstück und Gebäude besitzen eine lange und wechsel-volle Geschichte: Zu Zeiten des Römischen Reichs stand hier eine Basilika und im 15. Jahrhundert ein Stadtpalais, in dem der königliche Intendant Jean d'Arlatan adlige Gäste empfing. Später zur Militärbaracke degradiert, wurde aus dem Haus Ende der 1980er ein elegantes Hotel, das schließlich in den Besitz der Arles-affinen Kunstmäzenin Maja Hoffmann überging. Sie ließ den denkmalgeschützten Bau rundum renovieren – unter Regie von Jorge Pardo, amerikanischer Künstler mit kubanischen Wurzeln und Studio in Mexiko. Bekannt für seine „Gesamtkunstwerke", machte er auch aus dem Arlatan ein Unikat; eine ebenso exzentrische wie eklektische Adresse, die südamerikanische und südfranzösische Lebenskunst verbindet. So verlegte er auf einer Boden- und Wandfläche von 6000 Quadratmetern ein einzigartiges Mega-Mosaik – die fast zwei Milionen Fliesen in elf verschiedenen Formen und 18 Farbtönen wurden in einer stillgelegten Fabrik in Yucatán gebrannt, die für dieses Projekt wiedereröffnet wurde. Auch die Möbel im Retro-Stil,

gefertigt aus nachhaltig angebautem Guanacaste-Holz aus Costa Rica, sowie die fantasievollen Lampen und Kronleuchter sind eigene Entwürfe – ebenso wie die Gemälde, die sämtliche Türen und Räume schmücken und von Motiven Vincent van Goghs inspiriert sind. Auf einigen Bildern hat Pardo auch sich selbst oder die Hotelbesitzerin verewigt. Es macht Spaß, sie aufzuspüren – die Entdeckungsreise kann beginnen! ◆ Buchtipp: „Van Gogh. Briefe" von Johanna Gesina van Gogh-Bonger.

ANREISE *Im historischen Zentrum von Arles gelegen, 1 km vom Bahnhof entfernt (4 Std. im TGV nach Paris). Nächster Flughafen ist Marseille (70 km)* · **PREIS** *€–€€€* · **ZIMMER** *35 Zimmer (sowie 6 Zimmer mit Küche für „artists in residence" und 1 Gästehaus)* · **KÜCHE** *Das Restaurant serviert provenzalische und mediterrane Gerichte. Zudem gibt es eine schicke Cocktailbar* · **GESCHICHTE** *Nach dreijähriger Renovierung wurde das Hotel 2018 eröffnet* · **X-FAKTOR** *Design bis ins Detail: Selbst den Pool ziert ein Mosaik*

UN KALÉIDOSCOPE

L'histoire du terrain et du bâtiment est longue et mouvementée : une basilique se dressait ici sous l'Empire romain et, au XVe siècle, un hôtel particulier où l'intendant royal Jean d'Arlatan recevait de nobles hôtes. Transformée plus tard en caserne, la maison est devenue à la fin des années 1980 un hôtel élégant et finalement la propriété de Maja Hoffmann, mécène de la ville d'Arles. Elle a fait entièrement rénover le bâtiment classé, sous la direction de Jorge Pardo, un artiste américain d'origine cubaine qui possède un atelier au Mexique. Connu pour ses « œuvres d'art totales », il a également fait de l'Arlatan quelque chose d'exceptionnel, une adresse aussi excentrique qu'éclectique, qui marie l'art de vivre de l'Amérique du Sud et du midi de la France. Il a ainsi posé une méga-mosaïque unique en son genre sur 6 000 mètres carrés de sol et de mur – les presque deux millions de carreaux présentant onze formes et 18 couleurs différentes ont été cuits dans une usine désaffectée du Yucatan, rouverte pour ce projet. Les meubles de style rétro, fabriqués en bois de Guanacaste du Costa Rica cultivé

durablement, ainsi que les lampes et lustres pleins de fantaisie, sont également des créations personnelles – tout comme les peintures qui décorent toutes les portes et les chambres et sont inspirées de motifs de Vincent van Gogh. Pardo a également immortalisé sa personne ou la propriétaire de l'hôtel dans certains des tableaux. C'est amusant de les chercher… Partons à la découverte ! ◆ À lire : « Lettres à son frère Théo » de Vincent van Gogh.

ACCÈS *Dans le centre historique d'Arles, à 1 km de la gare (à 4 h de Paris en TGV). L'aéroport le plus proche est Marseille (70 km)* · **PRIX** *€–€€€* · **CHAMBRES** *35 chambres, 6 chambres avec cuisine pour les « artists in residence » et 1 maison d'hôtes* · **RESTAURATION** *Le restaurant propose des plats de la cuisine provençale et méditerranéenne. On trouve aussi ici un bar à cocktails très chic* · **HISTOIRE** *Après des travaux de rénovation qui ont duré trois ans, l'hôtel a ouvert ses portes en 2018* · **LES « PLUS »** *Le design se niche jusque dans les moindres détails : même la piscine est décorée d'une mosaïque*

LE CLOÎTRE

ARLES, PROVENCE, FRANCE

LE CLOÎTRE

16–22, rue du Cloître, 13200 Arles, France
Tel. + 33 488 091 000 · contact@hotel-cloitre.com
www.lecloitre.com

THE COLORS OF THE CAMARGUE

She loved Arles during her childhood, which she spent in the Camargue. Her father Luc, heir to the pharmaceutical giant Roche, donated to the local Van Gogh Foundation a headquarters in a former branch of the Banque de France. And with Luma Arles, she herself initiated one of the largest private arts projects in Europe – an interdisciplinary cultural center on a disused railway site, with a spectacular tower of glass and aluminium by Frank Gehry at its heart: the Swiss arts patron Maja Hoffmann and her family have made Arles one of France's leading centers of art. For exploring the museums and sights of the town, the best accommodation is the Hotel Le Cloître, which also belongs to Maja Hoffmann. The interior designer India Mahdavi renovated this former monastery in enchanting and light-hearted style, painting the walls in the region's shades of blue, green and ocher, laying wonderful mosaics and furnishing the rooms with design classics and imaginative details. A popular spot is the Épicerie du Cloître – a delicatessen and restaurant at one and the same time, which supplies southern specialities to hotel guests and passers-by from morning to evening, and possesses a lovely veranda beneath a hundred-year-old empress tree. Exclusively reserved for residents at Le Cloître is the roof garden, a place to sip a drink while enjoying a superb view of Arles that is as pretty as a picture. ◆ Book to pack: "Memoirs" by Frédéric Mistral.

DIRECTIONS *In the historic city center near the amphitheatre, a 10-minute walk from the rail station (4 hours from Paris by high-speed train); the nearest airport is Marseille (70 km/44 miles)* · RATES € · ROOMS *19 rooms* · FOOD *The menu in the Épicerie changes weekly, always based on fresh local ingredients. Simple but delicious!* · HISTORY *Some of the walls of the house date from the Middle Ages. India Mahdavi designed the hotel in 2012–13* · X-FACTOR *The personal, straightforward service*

DIE FARBEN DER CAMARGUE

Sie liebte Arles schon während ihrer Kindheit, die sie in der Camargue verbrachte. Ihr Vater Luc, Erbe des Pharmariesens Roche, spendierte der örtlichen Van-Gogh-Stiftung einen Stammsitz in der ehemaligen Filiale der Banque de France. Und sie selbst initiierte mit „Luma Arles" eines der größten privaten Kulturprojekte Europas – ein interdisziplinäres Kulturzentrum auf einem ausrangierten Bahngelände, dessen Herzstück ein aufsehenerregender Turm aus Glas und Aluminium von Frank Gehry ist: Die Schweizer Mäzenin Maja Hoffmann und ihre Familie haben Arles zu einem der kunstsinnigsten Orte Frankreichs gemacht. Wer die Museen und Sehenswürdigkeiten der Stadt entdecken möchte, wohnt am besten im Hotel Le Cloître, das ebenfalls Maja Hoffmann gehört. Die Interiordesignerin India Mahdavi hat das einstige Kloster zauberhaft und lebensfroh renoviert, die Wände in den Blau-, Grün- und Ockertönen der Region getüncht, herrliche Mosaike verlegt und die Zimmer mit Designklassikern sowie fantasievollen Details eingerichtet. Ein Lieblingsplatz ist die „Épicerie du Cloître" – Feinkostladen und Restaurant zugleich, das Hotelgäste und Passanten von morgens bis abends mit Spezialitäten des Südens versorgt und eine Bilderbuchveranda unter einem hundertjährigen Blauglockenbaum besitzt. Exklusiv für Bewohner des Le Cloître ist der Dachgarten – dort genießt man bei einem Drink eine herrliche Aussicht über Arles, so schön wie ein Gemälde. ◆ Buchtipp: „Kindheit und Jugend in der Provence" von Frédéric Mistral.

ANREISE *Im historischen Zentrum nahe dem Amphitheater gelegen. Der Bahnhof ist 10 Min. zu Fuß entfernt (4 Std. im TGV nach Paris), nächster Flughafen ist Marseille (70 km)* · **PREIS €** · **ZIMMER** *19 Zimmer* · **KÜCHE** *Das Menü der „Épicerie" wechselt wöchentlich und basiert immer auf frischen, lokalen Zutaten. Die Gerichte sind schlicht, aber köstlich!* · **GESCHICHTE** *Die ältesten Teile des Hauses stammen aus dem Mittelalter. India Mahdavi gestaltete das Hotel 2012/13 neu* · **X-FAKTOR** *Der persönliche, unkomplizierte Service*

LES COULEURS DE LA CAMARGUE

Elle aimait déjà Arles pendant son enfance, passée en Camargue. Son père Luc, héritier du géant pharmaceutique Roche, a fait don à la fondation locale Van Gogh d'une permanence dans l'ancienne succursale de la Banque de France. Et c'est elle qui a lancé « Luma Arles », un des plus grands projets culturels privés d'Europe – un centre culturel interdisciplinaire sur un site ferroviaire abandonné, dont le cœur est une spectaculaire tour en verre et en aluminium de Frank Gehry : la mécène suisse Maja Hoffmann et sa famille ont fait d'Arles un des lieux les plus sensibles à l'art en France. À ceux ou celles qui veulent découvrir les musées et les curiosités de la ville, on recommandera un séjour à l'hôtel Le Cloître, également propriété de Maja Hoffmann. L'architecte d'intérieur India Mahdavi a rénové de manière magique et joyeuse l'ancien monastère, peint à la chaux les murs dans les bleus, verts et ocres de la région, posé de magnifiques mosaïques et meublé les pièces avec des classiques du design et des détails inventifs. À la fois épicerie fine et restaurant, l'Épicerie du Cloître est un lieu recherché qui propose du matin au soir des spécialités méridionales aux clients de l'hôtel et aux passants et dont la véranda, sous un paulownia aux fleurs bleues centenaire, semble sortie d'un livre d'images. Le jardin sur le toit est réservé aux habitants du Cloître, vous pourrez déguster une boisson en profitant d'une vue magnifique sur Arles, aussi belle qu'une peinture. ◆ À lire : « Mes origines – Mémoires et récits » par Frédéric Mistral.

ACCÈS *Dans le centre historique près de l'amphithéâtre. La gare est à 10 min à pied (en TGV, on rejoint Paris en 4 h), l'aéroport le plus proche est à Marseille (70 km)* · **PRIX €** · **CHAMBRES** *19 chambres* · **RESTAURATION** *Le menu de « L'Épicerie », à base de produits frais locaux, change toutes les semaines. Les plats sont simples, mais délicieux !* · **HISTOIRE** *Les murs les plus anciens de la maison datent du Moyen Âge. India Mahdavi a aménagé l'hôtel en 2012/13* · **LES « PLUS »** *Le service personnel, sans chichis*

CHÂTEAU LA COSTE

LE PUY-SAINTE-RÉPARADE, PROVENCE, FRANCE

CHÂTEAU LA COSTE

2750, route de la Cride, 13610 Le Puy-Sainte-Réparade, France
Tel. +33 442 505 000 · reservations@villalacoste.com
www.villalacoste.com
www.chateau-la-coste.com

A MASTERPIECE

He wanted to create a place combining wine, art and architecture. Though this may sound simple, and though he himself is modest, the people whose support he gained for his project are big names: on his estate in Provence, the Irish businessman and art collector Patrick McKillen exhibits modern classics such as Louise Bourgeois' larger-than-lifesize spider made from bronze and steel, which seems to be creeping across a pool of water here. He invites his guests to exhibitions in a gallery designed by Tadao Andō, and to concerts in a music pavilion by Frank Gehry. Even his production premises for wine from organically cultivated grapes bear a famous signature: the two halls of corrugated aluminium are the work of Jean Nouvel. Almost every artist and every architect who is represented at Château La Coste has walked across the site and personally chosen the spot for his or her work. The collection is still by no means complete – it is intended to grow continuously through new installations and buildings. Visitors need plenty of time, so it is convenient that the estate possesses a hotel. Villa La Coste lies among vineyards, and accommodates guests in luxurious suites that are bathed in light, have a touch of industrial style, and are equipped with modern Provençal furnishings. At the gourmet restaurant Louison, designed in the same style, the wheel comes full circle: this is an act of homage to Louise Bourgeois, presenting as its centerpiece her hanging sculpture "The Couple", shining silver. ◆ Book to pack: "The Farm Théotime" by Henri Bosco.

DIRECTIONS *45 minutes from Marseille airport and 35 minutes from the train station in Aix-en-Provence* · **RATES** €€€€ · **ROOMS** *28 suites (for 2–4 guests), several with a private pool* · **FOOD** *Apart from from Louison with its fine Provençal menus, the hotel has a rustic restaurant, in which Francis Mallmann serves his Argentinian specialities from the grill. A Mediterranean restaurant with a lovely terrace is attached to Tadao Andō's art center* · **HISTORY** *The collection opened in 2011, the hotel in 2017* · **X-FACTOR** *The hotel spa, which uses natural extracts of products from Provence such as lavender, roses and jasmine*

EIN MEISTERWERK

Er wollte einen Ort schaffen, an dem Wein, Kunst und Architektur zusammenkommen. So einfach das klingt und so diskret er selbst ist, so groß sind die Namen, die er für sein Projekt gewinnen konnte: Der irische Unternehmer und Kunstsammler Patrick McKillen zeigt auf seinem Gut in der Provence moderne Klassiker wie Louise Bourgeois' überlebensgroße Spinne aus Bronze und Stahl, die hier über ein Wasserbecken zu wandeln scheint. Er lädt zu Ausstellungen in ein Zentrum, das Tadao Andō entworfen hat, und zu Konzerten in einen Musikpavillon von Frank Gehry. Selbst seine Kellerei für Wein aus biodynamischem Anbau trägt eine berühmte Handschrift – die zwei Produktionshallen aus gewelltem Aluminium stammen von Jean Nouvel. Fast jeder Künstler und jeder Architekt, der im Château La Coste vertreten ist, ist über das Gelände gewandert und hat persönlich den Platz ausgewählt, an dem sein Werk (ent)stehen sollte. Vollständig ist die Kollektion noch lange nicht – sie soll sich mit neuen Installationen sowie Bauten kontinuerlich weiterentwickeln. Besucher brauchen viel Zeit, und so trifft es sich gut, dass zum Anwesen auch ein Hotel gehört. Die Villa La Coste liegt mitten in den Weinbergen und beherbergt Gäste in luxuriösen, lichtdurchfluteten Suiten, die einen Hauch Industrieflair atmen und mit modernem provenzalischem Mobiliar eingerichtet sind. Im selben Stil ist das Gourmetrestaurant „Louison" designt, welches den Kreis schließt: Das Lokal ist eine Hommage an Louise Bourgeois und präsentiert als Herzstück deren silbrig glänzende Hängeskulptur „The Couple". ◆ Buchtipp: „Der Hof Theotime" von Henri Bosco.

ANREISE 45 Min. vom Flughafen Marseille und 35 Min. vom Bahnhof Aix-en-Provence entfernt · PREIS €€€€ · ZIMMER 28 Suiten (für 2–4 Gäste), einige mit Privatpool · KÜCHE Außer dem „Louison" mit feinen provenzalischen Menüs besitzt das Hotel ein rustikales Restaurant, in dem Francis Mallmann seine argentinischen Grillspezialitäten serviert. Dem Kunstzentrum von Tadao Andō angeschlossen ist ein mediterranes Lokal mit schöner Terrasse · GESCHICHTE Die Sammlung eröffnete 2011, das Hotel 2017 · X-FAKTOR Das Hotelspa, in dem natürliche Wirkstoffe der Provence verwendet werden, z. B. aus Lavendel, Rosen und Jasmin

UN CHEF-D'ŒUVRE

Il voulait créer un endroit où le vin, l'art et l'architecture seraient en présence. Cela paraît simple et lui-même est très discret, et pourtant de grands noms ont répondu à son appel : l'entrepreneur et collectionneur d'art irlandais Patrick McKillen présente dans son domaine provençal des classiques modernes tels l'araignée de Louise Bourgeois, plus grande que nature, en bronze et en acier, qui semble ici marcher sur les eaux d'un bassin. Il invite à des expositions dans un centre dessiné par Tadao Andō et à des concerts dans un pavillon de musique de Frank Gehry. Même sa cave qui renferme des vins issus de la culture biodynamique porte une signature célèbre – les deux salles de production en aluminium ondulé ont été conçues par Jean Nouvel. Presque tous les artistes et architectes représentés au château La Coste ont parcouru le site et ont personnellement choisi l'endroit où installer leurs œuvres. La collection est loin d'être complète – elle va continuer à évoluer avec de nouvelles installations et de nouveaux bâtiments. Les visiteurs ont besoin de beaucoup de temps, et c'est donc une bonne chose qu'un hôtel appartienne aussi à la propriété. L'hôtel Villa La Coste est situé au milieu des vignes et accueille les hôtes dans des suites luxueuses, inondées de lumière, qui affichent une touche industrielle et abritent un mobilier provençal moderne. Conçu dans le même style, le restaurant gastronomique « Louison » boucle la boucle : le restaurant est un hommage à Louise Bourgeois et sa pièce maîtresse est « The Couple », la sculpture suspendue argentée de celle-ci. ◆ À lire : « Le Mas Théotime » d'Henri Bosco.

ACCÈS À 45 min de l'aéroport de Marseille et à 35 min de la gare d'Aix-en-Provence · PRIX €€€€ · CHAMBRES 28 suites (pour 2–4 personnes), quelques-unes avec piscine privée · RESTAURATION À côté du « Louison » qui propose des plats raffinés de la cuisine provençale, l'hôtel possède un restaurant rustique dans lequel Francis Mallmann sert ses grillades argentines. Un restaurant de cuisine méditerranéenne disposant d'une belle terrasse est relié au centre artistique dessiné par Tadao Andō · HISTOIRE La collection a ouvert ses portes en 2011, l'hôtel en 2017 · LES « PLUS » Le spa de l'hôtel, dans lequel sont utilisées des substances naturelles de Provence, par exemple la lavande, la rose et le jasmin

HOTEL CIPRIANI

VENICE, ITALY

HOTEL CIPRIANI

Giudecca 10, 30133 Venice, Italy
Tel. + 39 41 240 801 · info.cip@belmond.com
www.belmond.com/hotelcipriani

A WORLD AFLOAT

"Streets flooded. Please advise." So said a telegram once sent from here by a humorous writer. But seriously, there is not much that can match the first sight of Venice. You should choose to arrive by boat: the ride along the Grand Canal, past palaces and churches, then turning into the lagoon of San Marco to see the sunlight glinting on the domes of the Doge's Palace, is a memorable one. The boat will bring you to Palazzo Vendramin, the 15th-century residence on one of the many islands that make up this ancient city. The Palazzo's beautiful arched windows frame one of the most romantic and famous views in the world: the front-row view of St. Mark's Square. With only a few suites, it is more akin to an elegant private home; however, it is part of the famed Belmond Hotel Cipriani, but a short stroll away, across the courtyard. And guests may share in all of the Cipriani's wealth of resources. Just a few minutes from its calm cloisters is a busier, noisier place. This special city of the past is quite like a magnet. Yet, off the main sightseeing trail, there is a quieter, slower Venice still to be glimpsed. ◆ Books to pack: "Death In Venice" by Thomas Mann and "A Venetian Reckoning" by Donna Leon.

DIRECTIONS *30 min by boat from Marco Polo airport* · **RATES** *€€€€* · **ROOMS** *16 rooms and suites at the Palazzo Vendramin and the Palazzetto, 82 rooms and suites at the Hotel Cipriani* · **FOOD** *The cooking at the Cipriani and Cip's Club is to die for. In the Oro Restaurant, Michelin star-winning chef Davide Bisetto serves up his imaginative creations* · **HISTORY** *It opened as a hotel in 1991, and the Palazzetto Nani Barbaro in 1998* · **X-FACTOR** *One of the most incomparable places in the world*

EINE WELT IM FLUSS

„Alle Straßen unter Wasser. Was ist zu tun?", lautete das Telegramm, das ein Schriftsteller mit Humor hier einst aufgab. Doch im Ernst: Der erste Anblick von Venedig lässt sich mit nichts vergleichen. Wenn es geht, sollte man in der Stadt mit dem Boot ankommen. Die Fahrt auf dem Canal Grande vorbei an Palazzi und Kirchen, der Blick in die Lagune von San Marco, wenn die Sonne über den Dogenpalast dahingleitet, ist unvergesslich. Mit dem Boot gelangt man auch zum Palazzo Vendramin, ein Anwesen aus dem 15. Jahrhundert, das auf einer der vielen Inseln Venedigs liegt. Von hier aus bietet sich – gerahmt durch die Bogenfenster des Palazzo – ein fantastischer Blick auf den Markusplatz, einer der schönsten, berühmtesten und romantischsten Ausblicke der Welt. Der Palazzo erinnert mit seinen wenigen Suiten eher an ein elegantes Privathaus als an ein Hotel. Doch ist er Teil des berühmten Belmond Hotel Cipriani, das sich in einem wenige Minuten dauernden Spaziergang quer über einen Innenhof erreichen lässt. Den Gästen des Palazzo stehen auch die vielfältigen Angebote des Cipriani zur Verfügung.

Nur wenige Minuten von der fast klösterlichen Ruhe und Beschaulichkeit entfernt, taucht man in ein bunteres und lauteres Leben ein. Venedig scheint eine Stadt aus der Vergangenheit zu sein, doch ihre Anziehungskraft ist bis heute ungebrochen. Wie schön, dass es neben den typischen Touristenattraktionen noch ein leiseres und ruhigeres Venedig zu entdecken gibt. ◆ Buchtipps: „Der Tod in Venedig" von Thomas Mann und „Venezianische Scharade" von Donna Leon.

ANREISE *30 Min. Anfahrt mit dem Boot vom Flughafen Marco Polo ·* PREIS *€€€€ ·* ZIMMER *16 Zimmer und Suiten im Palazzo Vendramin und im Palazzetto, 82 Zimmer und Suiten im Hotel Cipriani ·* KÜCHE *Das Essen im Cipriani und Cip's Club ist himmlisch. Die fantasievollen Kreationen von Davide Bisetto im Restaurant Oro wurden mit einem Michelin-Stern ausgezeichnet ·* GESCHICHTE *Der Palazzo Vendramin aus dem 15. Jahrhundert öffnete 1991 als Hotel, der Palazzetto Nani Barbaro 1998 ·* X-FAKTOR *Einer der unvergleichlichsten Orte der Welt*

ENTRE TERRE ET EAU

« Rues inondées. Que faire ? » Tel est le message télégraphique qu'envoya un visiteur de Venise qui ne manquait pas d'humour ! Trêve de plaisanteries ; rien ou presque n'égale l'impact de la première vision de Venise. Arrivez de préférence à Venise par bateau. Le trajet le long du Grand Canal et de ses palais et églises, l'entrée dans la lagune de Saint-Marc pour voir le soleil scintiller sur les toits du Palais des Doges, est tout à fait mémorable. Le bateau vous amènera au Palazzo Vendramin. Cette résidence du XVe siècle se dresse sur l'une des nombreuses îles qui forment la ville ancienne. Le Palazzo donne sur la place Saint-Marc ; ses superbes fenêtres en plein cintre encadrent l'une des places les plus romantiques et célèbres du monde. N'abritant que quelques suites, il évoque une élégante résidence privée, bien qu'il fasse partie de l'illustre Belmond Hotel Cipriani, situé seulement à quelques pas, de l'autre côté de la cour. Ses hôtes peuvent profiter de tout ce que le Cipriani a à offrir. À quelques minutes à peine de

la tranquillité de ses murs, s'étend une place bruyante et fort animée. Cette ville d'un autre temps est en effet un véritable aimant touristique. Néanmoins, au-delà des sentiers battus, se cache une Venise plus nonchalante et sereine. ◆ À lire : « La Mort à Venise » de Thomas Mann et « Un Vénitien anonyme » de Donna Leon.

ACCÈS *À 30 min de bateau de l'aéroport Marco Polo ·* PRIX *€€€€ ·* CHAMBRES *16 chambres et suites dans le Palazzo Vendramin et le Palazzetto, 82 chambres et suites à l'hôtel Cipriani ·* RESTAURATION *On se ferait naufragé volontaire pour la cuisine du Cipriani et du Cip's Club. Au restaurant Oro, le chef étoilé au Michelin Davide Bisetto sert ses créations pleines de fantaisie ·* HISTOIRE *Le Palazzo Vendramin a été construit au XVe siècle. Il a ouvert sous forme d'hôtel en 1991, le Palazzetto Nani Barbaro en 1998 ·* LES « PLUS » *L'un des lieux les plus inoubliables du monde*

CASA IRIS

ORBETELLO, TUSCANY, ITALY

CASA IRIS

Corso Italia 3, 58015 Orbetello, Italy
Tel. + 39 392 529 8010 . casairisorbetello@gmail.com
www.casairisorbetello.com
Open from April to October

A NEW HOME

From Manhattan to the Maremma: the contrast could hardly be greater, but sometimes life simply needs a new idea, new impulses, new inspiration. Which is why a 500-year-old palazzo in the heart of Orbetello triggered a move by the stylist James Valeri and his husband Matthew Adams. James' grandmother had once lived in this building – and today it houses a boutique bed & breakfast whose name is a tribute to this former resident. James and Matthew spent two years converting the historic house, for which they called on high-calibre support: Maria Rosaria Basileo, who has restored such legendary buildings as the Sistine Chapel and Villa Borghese, uncovered the wonderful frescoes on the ceilings and walls, and the architect Giorgia Cerulli composed the elegant, eclectic style of the suites. Decorated in pastel shades, the rooms are showcases for Italian design classics from 1930 to 1970, effectively combined with Art Nouveau accessories and superb chandeliers – the owners went all over Italy to assemble these remarkable retro furnishings. The chic style appears in the blue-gray kitchen, too, where guests meet for breakfast. Hearty regional treats easily see them through the day, for which the hosts provide excellent sightseeing tips – they both know the Maremma as well as they once knew Manhattan.

◆ Book to pack: "Michelangelo" by Irving Stone.

DIRECTIONS *In the pedestrian zone of Orbetello, a charming port 136 km/85 miles from Rome airport* · **RATES** *€€–€€€* · **ROOMS** *3 suites (one of them for up to 3 persons), all with their own bathroom* · **FOOD** *For lunch and dinner there are many restaurants within walking distance* · **HISTORY** *Opened in early 2018* · **X-FACTOR** *Design and dolce vita are united here*

EINE NEUE HEIMAT

Von Manhattan in die Maremma: Der Gegensatz könnte kaum größer sein – doch manchmal braucht das Leben einfach eine neue Idee, neue Impulse, neue Inspiration. Und so gab ein 500 Jahre alter Palazzo im Herzen von Orbetello den Anstoß für den Umzug des Stylisten James Valeri und seines Ehemanns Matthew Adams. Einst hatte in diesem Gebäude James' Großmutter Iris gelebt – heute birgt es ein Boutique Bed & Breakfast, dessen Name eine Hommage an die ehemalige Bewohnerin ist. Zwei Jahre investierten James und Matthew in den Umbau des historischen Hauses und holten sich dafür hochrangige Unterstützung: Maria Rosaria Basileo, die legendäre Bauten wie die Sixtinische Kapelle sowie die Villa Borghese restaurierte, legte die wunderschönen Fresken an Decken und Wänden frei, und die Architektin Giorgia Cerulli komponierte den elegant-eklektischen Stil der Suiten. In Pastelltönen gehalten, setzen die Räume italienische Designklassiker der Jahrzehnte 1930 bis 1970 in Szene und kombinieren sie effektvoll mit Art-nouveau-Accessoires sowie prächtigen Leuchtern – die Besitzer reisten durch ganz Italien, um dieses außergewöhnliche Retromobiliar zusammenzutragen. Chic und Stil reichen bis in die taubenblaue Küche, in der sich die Gäste zum Frühstück treffen. Die reichhaltigen regionalen Köstlichkeiten bringen einen locker durch den Tag, für den die Hausherren ausgezeichnete Sightseeing-Tipps geben – die beiden kennen die Maremma so gut wie einst Manhattan. ◆ Buchtipp: „Michelangelo" von Irving Stone.

ANREISE *In der Fußgängerzone der charmanten Hafenstadt Orbetello gelegen, 136 km vom Flughafen Rom entfernt ·* PREIS *€€–€€€ ·* ZIMMER *3 Suiten (davon eine für bis zu 3 Personen), alle mit eigenem Bad ·* KÜCHE *Für Mittag- und Abendessen gibt es in Gehweite zahlreiche Restaurants ·* GESCHICHTE *Im Frühjahr 2018 eröffnet ·* X-FAKTOR *Hier treffen sich Design und Dolce Vita*

UN NOUVEAU PAYS

Entre Manhattan et la Maremme, le contraste ne pourrait être plus grand – mais parfois dans la vie, il suffit d'une idée nouvelle, d'un élan nouveau, d'inspirations inattendues. C'est ainsi qu'un palazzo vieux de cinq siècles au cœur d'Orbetello a amené le styliste James Valeri et son mari Matthew Adams à déménager. La grand-mère de James, Iris, a vécu autrefois dans ce bâtiment qui abrite aujourd'hui une boutique-hôtel bed & breakfast dont le nom lui rend hommage. Pendant deux ans, James et Matthew ont investi dans la reconstruction de la maison historique et ont obtenu un soutien de haut niveau : Maria Rosaria Basileo, qui a restauré des bâtiments mythiques tels que la chapelle Sixtine et la Villa Borghèse, a dégagé les fresques splendides ornant les plafonds et les murs, et l'architecte Giorgia Cerulli a créé le style élégant et éclectique des suites. Les pièces aux tons pastel mettent en valeur les classiques du design italien des années 1930 à 1970 associés à des accessoires Art nouveau et de magnifiques lustres – les propriétaires ont sillonné l'Italie pour assembler ce mobilier rétro exceptionnel. Le chic et le style s'étendent jusque dans la cuisine d'un bleu gris poudré, où les invités se retrouvent pour le petit déjeuner. Les spécialités régionales consistantes vous donneront de l'énergie pour la journée, que vous passerez en tirant profit des excellents conseils touristiques de vos hôtes : ils connaissent la Maremme aussi bien qu'ils connaissaient Manhattan autrefois. ◆ À lire : « La Vie ardente de Michel-Ange » d'Irving Stone.

ACCÈS *Dans la zone piétonnière de la charmante ville portuaire Orbetello, à 136 km de l'aéroport de Rome ·* PRIX *€€–€€€ ·* CHAMBRES *3 suites (l'une peut abriter jusqu'à 3 personnes), toutes avec salle de bains ·* RESTAURATION *De nombreux restaurants à proximité où l'on peut déjeuner et dîner ·* HISTOIRE *La maison a ouvert ses portes au printemps 2018 ·* LES « PLUS » *La rencontre du design et de la dolce vita*

HOTEL AIRE DE BARDENAS

TUDELA, NAVARRE, SPAIN

HOTEL AIRE DE BARDENAS

Ctra. De Ejea, 15 km, 31500 Tudela, Spain
Tel: + 34 948 116 666 · info@hotelairedebardenas.com
www.airedebardenas.com

LIFE ON MARS?

From a distance, the cube-shaped buildings with their aluminium façades that form the hotel complex, look like a futuristic colony; the reddish sand, characteristic of the barren landscape of Navarra in northern Spain, does the rest; or as David Bowie puts it in his song: Is there life on Mars? In the one-storey complex there is a total of 22 rooms and suites – guaranteeing a generous ceiling height. In addition, the individual houses are uniquely aligned to the sun and the line of the horizon, so as to create the illusion that you are in a luxurious hermitage. It's a dream that you can lose yourself in at any time, in the cool shade of the restaurant or out on the patio. The seemingly barren land of Navarra is a wine-growing region of worldwide renown, and the fertile farmland of the neighbouring region of Ribera is viewed by Spanish gourmets as a vegetable paradise. The lettuce hearts from nearby Tudela are a special delicacy! The mid-century design classics by Charles Eames found here show off their pioneering shapes, in front of the metal cubes in the red dust. Add to this the starry sky, and you'll feel ten thousand light years from home. ◆ Book to pack: "The House of Bernarda Alba" by Federico Garcia Lorca.

DIRECTIONS *40 minutes' drive north of the airport in Zaragoza, 2 hours' drive from Bilbao or Biarritz* · RATES *€€* · ROOMS *22 rooms, some with private patios or views over the desert of the Bardenas Reales Natural Park and Biosphere* · FOOD *Cooked with vegetables from the hotel's own garden; the focus is on vegetarian dishes. Victoria Beckham's favorite dish is zucchini strips fried with garlic* · HISTORY *The hotel was built by Mónica Rivera and Emiliano López and opened in 2007* · X-FACTOR *Star-gazing in the clear desert air*

LIFE ON MARS?

Von Weitem wirken die würfelförmigen Gebäude mit ihren Aluminiumfassaden, aus denen sich der Hotelkomplex zusammensetzt, wie eine futuristische Kolonie; der rötliche Sand, charakteristisch für die karge Landschaft der Navarra im Norden Spaniens, tut sein Übriges, oder wie David Bowie singt: „Is there Life on Mars?" In den einstöckigen Häusern sind insgesamt 22 Zimmer und Suiten untergebracht – was eine wunderbare Deckenhöhe garantiert. Zudem sind die einzelnen Häuser individuell an Sonnenstand und Horizontverlauf ausgerichtet, sodass die Illusion entsteht, man befände sich in einer luxuriösen Eremitage. Ein Traum, der sich im schattigen Restaurant, wahlweise auch auf dessen Terrasse, zu jeder Zeit zerstreuen lässt. Der vermeintlich karge Landstrich der Navarra ist ein Weinanbaugebiet von weltweitem Renommee, und das fruchtbare Ackerland der benachbarten Region Ribera wird von spanischen Feinschmeckern als Gemüseparadies gehandelt. Besonders die Salatherzen aus dem nahen Tudela sind eine Delikatesse! Die klassischen Midcentury-Designklassiker von Charles Eames stellen gerade hier, vor den Metallkuben im roten Staub, ihre zukunftsweisende Formgebung unter Beweis. Wenn dann noch der Sternenhimmel angeknipst wird, fühlt man sich zehntausend Lichtjahre von zu Hause entfernt. ◆ Buchtipp: „Bernarda Albas Haus" von Federico García Lorca.

ANREISE *40 Min. Fahrt nördlich vom Flughafen in Saragossa, 2 Std. Fahrt von Bilbao oder Biarritz* · PREIS *€€* · ZIMMER *22 Zimmer, teils mit eigenem Patio oder Aussichten in die Wüste des Bardenas-Reales-Nationalparks und -Biosphärenreservats* · KÜCHE *Es wird mit Gemüse aus dem hauseigenen Garten gekocht, der Schwerpunkt liegt dabei auf vegetarischen Gerichten. Victoria Beckhams Lieblingsgericht sind die mit Knoblauch gebratenen Zucchinistreifen* · GESCHICHTE *Das Hotel wurde von Mónica Rivera und Emiliano López gebaut und 2007 eröffnet* · X-FAKTOR *Sterneschauen bei klarer Wüstenluft*

LIFE ON MARS ?

De loin, les maisons cubiques aux façades en aluminium qui composent le complexe hôtelier font penser à une colonie futuriste ; le rouge du sable, typique de ce paysage aride de Navarre, dans le Nord de l'Espagne, fait le reste, ou comme le chante David Bowie : Is there Life on Mars ? Les maisons d'un étage abritent 22 chambres et suites — pour une superbe hauteur sous plafond garantie. Elles sont orientées différemment selon la position du soleil et la ligne de l'horizon, ce qui donne l'illusion de se trouver dans un luxueux ermitage. Le rêve est dissipé dès le premier instant dans le restaurant ombragé, ou au choix sur sa terrasse : la contrée apparemment pauvre de Navarre est en réalité un vignoble de renommée mondiale, et les terres agricoles fertiles de la région voisine de Ribera sont considérées par les gourmets espagnols comme le paradis des légumes — les cœurs de salade de la ville toute proche de Tudela en particulier sont un mets de choix ! Les classiques du design Midcentury de Charles Eames prouvent ici mieux que nulle part ailleurs, dans la poussière rouge devant les cubes métalliques, le caractère futuriste de leurs formes. Si en plus le ciel allume toutes ses étoiles, on se sent à dix mille années-lumière de chez soi. ◆ À lire : « La Maison de Bernarda Alba » de Federico Garcia Lorca.

ACCÈS *À 40 min de route au nord de l'aéroport de Saragosse, 2 h de route de Bilbao ou Biarritz* · PRIX *€€* · CHAMBRES *22 chambres, certaines avec patio ou vues sur le désert du parc national des Bardenas Reales et sa biosphère* · RESTAURATION *La cuisine est faite avec des légumes du jardin et met l'accent sur les plats végétariens. Le plat préféré de Victoria Beckham sont les rubans de courgettes sautés à l'ail* · HISTOIRE *L'hôtel a été construit par Mónica Rivera et Emiliano López et ouvert en 2007* · LES « PLUS » *Regarder les étoiles dans l'air clair du désert*

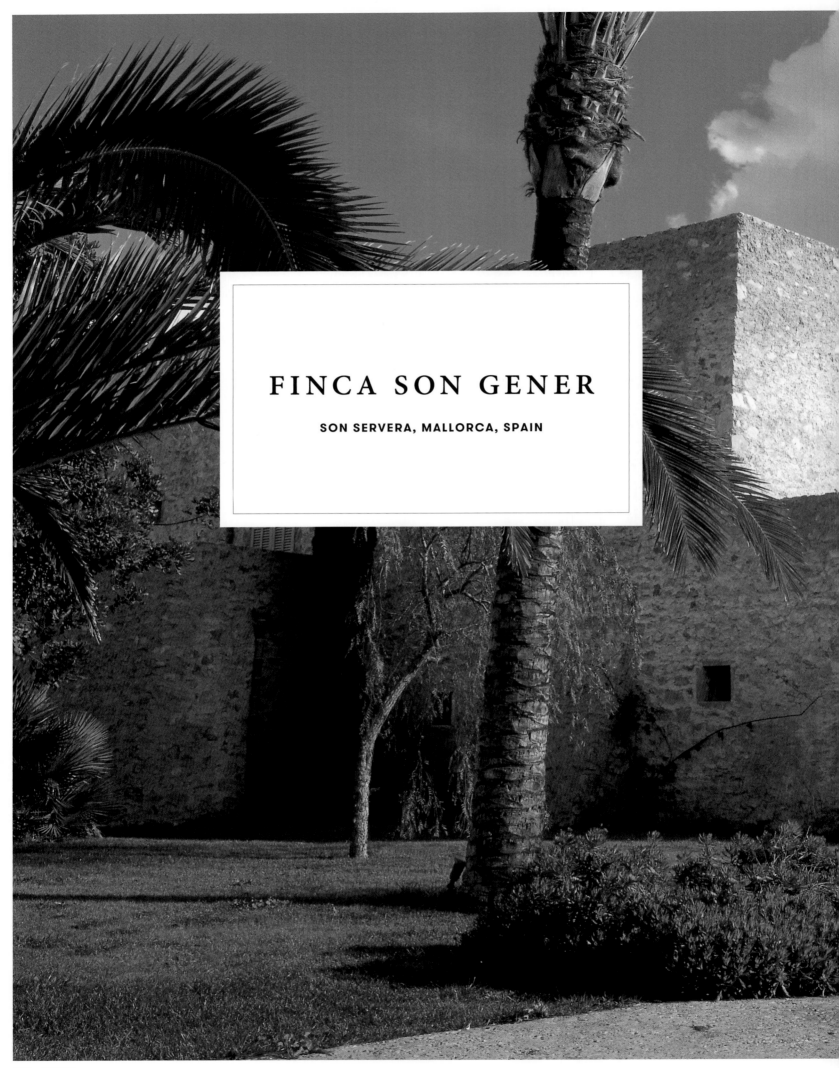

FINCA SON GENER

SON SERVERA, MALLORCA, SPAIN

FINCA SON GENER

Cta. Vella Son Servera-Artà, 07550 Son Servera, Mallorca, Spain
Tel: + 34 971 183 612 · hotel@songener.com
www.songener.com

SILENCE IS GOLDEN

Rural life has many rewards; one of the best is silence. Although the crowing of a rooster or the bleating of sheep may break that silence now and then, the peace and quiet that rules here is a treat in our noisy world. On the island of Mallorca, there is the chance to lead a simple country life for a few days. Some of the most beautiful places here are set in idyllic landscapes just near the coast, and often hidden behind thick natural stone walls. The country estate of Son Gener is one of these havens. Built in the 18th century, and used for making oils and grains, it has been totally restored. The classic finca – farm – is on the eastern side of the island, on the brow of a small hill, with a view of the village, sea, and mountains. Surrounded by green fields, olive and almond trees, this is a dream domain to bask in. While the estate's simple style is in keeping with its tranquil backdrop, it has been refurbished with skill. The soft rich colors that make up the interiors are in themselves conducive to a sense of calm. The elegant house calls to mind the patrician life of past days. Those who are privileged to be guests here will be content with their choice for a pastoral interlude. ◆ Book to pack: "Goya" by Lion Feuchtwanger.

DIRECTIONS *Between the towns of Son Servera and Artà, 70 km/44 miles east from Palma de Mallorca, 20 km/12 miles northeast from Manacor ·* **RATES** *€€ ·* **ROOMS** *10 suites ·* **FOOD** *On request, Mallorcan dishes made with homegrown organic produce are served ·* **HISTORY** *Built in the 18th century, the finca was turned into a hotel in 1998 ·* **X-FACTOR** *Outdoor and indoor serenity*

HIMMLISCHE RUHE

Das Landleben hat viele Vorzüge, aber einer der größten ist die Stille. Und auch wenn sie gelegentlich durch das Krähen eines Hahns oder das Blöken eines Schafs unterbrochen wird, herrscht doch meist Ruhe und Frieden – ein Luxus in unserer lauten Welt. Auf der Insel Mallorca haben Sie Gelegenheit, für einige Tage dem einfachen Landleben zu frönen. Einige der schönsten Unterkünfte finden sich hier inmitten idyllischer Landschaften nahe der Küste, oft versteckt hinter dicken Mauern aus Naturstein. Unter ihnen ist auch der Landsitz von Son Gener, eine klassische Finca, wie hier die Bauernhöfe genannt werden. Er liegt auf der Ostseite der Insel auf der Kuppe eines kleinen Hügels. Umgeben von grünen Feldern, Olivenhainen und Mandelbäumen finden Sie hier ein traumhaftes Urlaubsziel. Das im 18. Jahrhundert ursprünglich für die Öl- und Getreideproduktion gebaute Haus wurde komplett und mit großem Können renoviert. Davon zeugt der einfache Stil des Hauses, welcher sich harmonisch in die Umgebung einpasst. Zur allgemeinen Atmosphäre der Ruhe tragen die sanften, satten Farben im Hausinneren bei. Das elegante Haus weckt Erinnerungen an das Leben des gehobenen Bürgertums in früheren Zeiten. Wer das Privileg genießt, an diesem Ort Gast zu sein, wird mit seiner Wahl dieser ländlichen Oase mehr als zufrieden sein. ◆ Buchtipp: „Goya" von Lion Feuchtwanger.

ANREISE *Zwischen Son Servera und Artà, 70 km östlich von Palma, 20 km nordöstlich von Manacor* · PREIS *€€* · ZIMMER *10 Suiten* · KÜCHE *Auf Anfrage werden inseltypische Gerichte mit Zutaten aus eigenem biologischem Anbau serviert* · GESCHICHTE *Das Gebäude stammt aus dem 18. Jahrhundert und ist seit 1998 Hotel* · X-FAKTOR *Entspannte Atmosphäre in Haus und Umgebung*

LE SILENCE EST D'OR

La vie à la campagne a de nombreux avantages, en particulier le silence. Dans notre monde bruyant, cette paix et cette tranquillité, seulement interrompues de temps à autre par le cri d'un coq ou le bêlement d'un mouton, constituent un plaisir authentique. Dans l'île de Majorque, on peut, le temps d'un séjour, goûter à la vie campagnarde simple. Ici, certaines des plus belles villégiatures se cachent souvent derrière d'épais murs de pierre, dans des cadres idylliques, à proximité du littoral. Le domaine de Son Gener est l'un de ces havres de paix. Construit au XVIIIᵉ siècle, à l'origine destiné au pressage de l'huile et à la culture des céréales, il a été entièrement restauré. Cette finca (ferme) traditionnelle est située dans la partie orientale de l'île, au sommet d'une petite colline. Entourée de champs verdoyants, d'oliviers et d'amandiers, c'est un lieu de détente rêvé. Si le style simple du domaine s'harmonise avec son cadre rustique, celui-ci a été rénové avec goût. Les couleurs riches et douces des intérieurs favorisent l'impression de sérénité. L'élégante maison principale évoque la vie patricienne d'antan. Les privilégiés qui auront la chance de séjourner à Son Gener seront ravis du choix de leur interlude champêtre. ◆ À lire : « Goya » de Lion Feuchtwanger.

ACCÈS *Entre Son Servera et Artà, à 70 km à l'est de Palma, à 20 km au nord-est de Manacor* · PRIX *€€* · CHAMBRES *10 suites* · RESTAURATION *Sur demande, plats majorquins préparés avec des produits bio cultivés sur place* · HISTOIRE *Construit au XVIIIᵉ siècle, le bâtiment est un hôtel depuis 1998* · LES « PLUS » *Sérénité intérieure et extérieure*

POUSADA DE
AMARES

AMARES, PORTUGAL

POUSADA DE AMARES

Santa Maria do Bouro, 4720-633 Amares, Portugal
Tel: + 351 25 882 175 1 · reservas@pousadasofportugal.com
www.pousadasofportugal.com/pousadas/amares/

ARCHITECTURE MEETS NATURE

The former Cistercian monastery dating from the 12th century was rebuilt to plans by Pritzker Prize winner Eduardo Souto de Moura in the 1990s. With their strict asceticism and spirituality, their art and craft, the Cistercians were one of the most influential religious orders in the Middle Ages. They created monasteries of sublime austerity, and religious buildings to foster mental clarity and purity. Where monks once lived in barren cells, guests at Pousada de Amares now have minimalist rooms and suites at their disposal. Huge floor-to-ceiling windows provide views over the mountains. The medieval building still retains its solidity and beautiful proportions, which even now instill a sense of shelter. But a sensitive reworking of the foundations has removed any sense of severity. This is particularly evident in the stairwells. The sculptural elegance of the raw stone has been laid bare and, from a haven of silence, a temple of peace has been created. The furnishing is simply accentuated by the classic "model 209" chair by Thonet, which looks as if it had been specially created for the stone vaults of the restaurant. Le Corbusier favored this classic 1900 design for his sculptural concrete architecture. At dinner there, when the reflection of the flickering candles dances over the 800-year-old stone pillars, a magical and truly modern effect is produced.
◆ Book to pack: "The Gospel According to Jesus Christ" by José Saramago.

DIRECTIONS *79 km/49 miles north of the airport in Porto between Braga, the religious capital of Portugal, and Peneda-Gerês National Park ·* RATES *€–€€ ·* ROOMS *32 rooms including 2 suites ·* FOOD *A restaurant serves regional specialties. In the bar and on the terrace with views of the mountains you can enjoy the excellent local Vinho Verde ·* HISTORY *The monastery was built in the 12th century by the Cistercians, rebuilt between 1994–97 by Eduardo Souto de Moura and then opened as a Pousada hotel ·* X-FACTOR *The magnificent architecture and landscape*

ARCHITEKTUR TRIFFT NATUR

Das ehemalige Zisterzienserkloster aus dem 12. Jahrhundert wurde nach Plänen des Pritzker-Preisträgers Eduardo Souto de Moura in den 1990er-Jahren umgebaut. Mit ihrer strengen Spiritualität und Askese, Technik und Handwerk wurden die Zisterzienser im Hochmittelalter zu einem der einflussreichsten Orden. Sie schufen Klöster von erhabener Schmucklosigkeit und Sakralbauten für geistige Klarheit und Reinheit. Wo einst Mönche in kargen Zellen lebten, stehen den Gästen der Pousada de Amares nun minimalistisch eingerichtete Zimmer und Suiten zur Verfügung. Riesige bodentiefe Fenster geben den Blick frei auf die Berge. Die Wuchtigkeit und schönen Proportionen des mittelalterlichen Bauwerks, die für uns heute noch etwas Schützendes haben, sind dem Gebäude belassen worden. Doch wurde ihnen durch die sensible Neuaufteilung der Grundrisse jegliche Schwere genommen. Dies zeigt sich insbesondere in den Treppenhäusern. Freigelegt wurde die Eleganz des rohen Steins. Aus einem Hort des Schweigens wurde ein Tempel der Ruhe gemacht. Der Möblierung bleibt hier lediglich noch die Aufgabe zu akzentuieren, der klassische Stuhl „Modell 209" von Thonet wirkt wie geschaffen für die steinernen Gewölbe des Restaurants. Schon Le Corbusier favorisierte diesen Klassiker aus dem Jahr 1900 für seine skulpturale Betonarchitektur. Bei einem Dinner, wenn der Widerschein flackernder Kerzen an den 800 Jahre alten Steinsäulen tanzt, ergibt sich ein magischer, wahrhaft moderner Effekt. ◆ Buchtipp: „Das Evangelium nach Jesus Christus" von José Saramago.

ANREISE 79 km nördlich vom Flughafen in Porto zwischen Braga, der religiösen Hauptstadt Portugals, und dem Peneda-Gerês-Nationalpark gelegen · PREIS €–€€ · ZIMMER 32 Zimmer, davon 2 Suiten · KÜCHE Ein Restaurant serviert Spezialitäten der Region. In der Bar und auf der Terrasse mit Ausblicken auf die Berge genießt man den exzellenten, hiesigen Vinho Verde · GESCHICHTE Das Kloster wurde im 12. Jahrhundert von den Zisterziensern gebaut, 1994 bis 1997 von Eduardo Souto de Moura umgebaut und dann als Pousada-Hotel eröffnet · X-FAKTOR Die großartige Architektur und Landschaft!

SYMBIOSE ENTRE ARCHITECTURE ET NATURE

L'ancien couvent cistercien du XIIe siècle a été transformé dans les années 1990 d'après des plans de l'architecte lauréat du prix Pritzker Eduardo Souto de Moura. Les cisterciens, leur spiritualité sévère et leur ascèse, leur travail et leur artisanat, étaient l'un des ordres les plus influents pendant le haut Moyen Âge. Ils ont construit des couvents d'une simplicité et d'un dépouillement sublimes, ainsi que des bâtiments sacrés pour la clarté et la pureté de l'âme. Les austères cellules des moines d'autrefois sont aujourd'hui des chambres et des suites au mobilier minimaliste, à la disposition des clients de la Pousada de Amares. D'immenses fenêtres au ras du sol ouvrent une vue parfaitement dégagée sur les montagnes. L'imposant édifice moyenâgeux aux belles proportions a été conservé, il a pour nous aujourd'hui quelque chose de secret. Le redécoupage plein de sensibilité lui a cependant pris toute gravité, comme on le voit notamment aux escaliers. L'élégance sculpturale de la pierre brute a été dégagée et le havre du silence a fait place à un sanctuaire du calme. Le mobilier n'a été placé que pour accentuer encore le caractère de l'endroit : la chaise classique « 209 » de Thonet semble comme faite pour les voûtes de pierre du restaurant. Le Corbusier lui aussi avait privilégié ce modèle classique de 1900 pour son architecture sculpturale de béton. Les dîners à la lueur vacillante des bougies qui danse sur les colonnes de pierre vieilles de 800 ans s'y déroulent dans une atmosphère magique, mais véritablement moderne. ◆ À lire : « L'Évangile selon Jésus-Christ » de José Saramago.

ACCÈS À 79 km au nord de l'aéroport de Porto, entre Braga, la capitale religieuse du Portugal, et le parc national Peneda-Gerês · PRIX €–€€ · CHAMBRES 32 chambres, dont 2 suites · RESTAURATION Un restaurant sert des spécialités régionales. On peut déguster l'excellent vinho verde local au bar et sur la terrasse avec vue sur les montagnes · HISTOIRE Le couvent a été construit au XIIe siècle par les cisterciens, transformé de 1994 à 1997 par Eduardo Souto de Moura et ouvert en tant qu'hôtel Pousada · LES « PLUS » Architecture et paysage fantastiques !

PALACE HOTEL
DA CURIA

TAMENGOS, PORTUGAL

PALACE HOTEL
DA CURIA

3780-541 Curia, Tamengos, Portugal
Tel: + 351 231 510 300 · curia@almeidahotels.pt
www.almeidahotels.pt/en/hotel-coimbra

SOMEWHERE IN TIME

In the 1920s, this was a splendid new hotel. One of the last grand Art Nouveau buildings in Europe, it was quite the most stylish place when it first welcomed guests through its doors. It was set in magnificent gardens, in an elegant Portuguese spa town; one to which high-society people came to take the so-called healing waters. Luckily, the Palace Hotel da Curia is as lovely now as it was back then. Time seems to have stood still here. The atmosphere is much as it used to be. Although it has been restored, you can see what it must have been like a century ago. Wisely, little has been changed; it has been kept looking much as it did in the old days. New comforts have been added, but all the chic of that golden era remains. Yet this stately old hotel is still a new landmark in a region that is steeped in history. The Beiras near the Atlantic Ocean is a lesser known part of Portugal and rather off the beaten track. Its surroundings range from mountains to lush valleys, from quiet villages to long, curving beaches. Though it may be short on attention, it is rich in variety. ◆ Book to pack: "Journey to Portugal" by José Saramago.

DIRECTIONS *20 km/12 miles north of Coimbra, 2 hours north from Lisbon, 1 hour south from Porto* · **RATES** *€–€€* · **ROOMS** *100 rooms* · **FOOD** *Local specialities and classic international cuisine* · **HISTORY** *Built in the early 1920s, the Palace Hotel da Curia opened in 1926. Complete renovation, concluded in 2008, reinforced the historical character of the place and added a boutique spa* · **X-FACTOR** *Belle Époque flair*

EINE ANDERE ZEIT

Erbaut in den 1920er-Jahren, gehörte das Hotel zu den letzten großen Jugendstilbauten Europas und galt, als es seine ersten Gäste willkommen hieß, als Verkörperung wahren Stils. Es lag in einer prachtvollen Gartenanlage in einem eleganten Kurort, wo sich die High Society an den heilenden Quellen labte. Glücklicherweise scheint im Palace Hotel da Curia die Zeit stehen geblieben zu sein, sodass man förmlich die zauberhafte Atmosphäre vergangener Tage spürt. Obwohl das Hotel inzwischen renoviert wurde, kann man sich genau vorstellen, wie es hier vor fast einem Jahrhundert zuging. Denn es wurde klugerweise nur wenig verändert. Natürlich ist moderner Komfort hinzugekommen, doch das Flair des Goldenen Zeitalters blieb erhalten. Und man darf eines nicht vergessen: Inmitten dieser durch und durch historischen Landschaft ist das

ehrwürdige alte Hotel immer noch ein relativ neues Wahrzeichen. Die Landschaft Beiras an der Atlantikküste Portugals gehört zu den weniger bekannten Regionen, in die sich nicht jeder „verirrt". Dabei ist sie eine der abwechslungsreichsten des Landes. Hier finden sich Bergzüge neben üppig begrünten Tälern, stille Dörfchen und lange Strände. ◆ Buchtipp: „Hoffnung im Alentejo" von José Saramago.

ANREISE *20 km nördlich von Coimbra, 2 Std. nördlich von Lissabon und 1 Std. südlich von Porto entfernt* · **PREIS** *€–€€* · **ZIMMER** *100 Zimmer* · **KÜCHE** *Lokale Spezialitäten und klassische internationale Küche* · **GESCHICHTE** *Erbaut in den 1920er-Jahren, eröffnet 1926* · **X-FAKTOR** *Flair der Belle Époque*

RÉMINISCENCES

Dans les années 1920, c'était un hôtel Art nouveau flambant neuf ; l'un de ces établissements élégants où se côtoyait l'élite européenne. Entouré d'un magnifique jardin, il se dressait dans une ville portugaise alors très sélect, réputée pour ses eaux thermales curatives. Par bonheur, le Palace Hotel da Curia a su garder son charme et son atmosphère d'antan. Ici, le temps semble s'être arrêté. Bien que l'hôtel ait été restauré, il a fort heureusement subi peu de changements et offre la même ambiance qui y régnait il y a près de cent ans. Si l'on y trouve aujourd'hui tout le confort moderne, il a su conserver le cachet typique de la Belle Époque. Désormais d'un autre siècle, ce palace majestueux reste néanmoins une création encore bien jeune dans cette région gorgée d'histoire.

Beiras sur la côte atlantique est une des contrées les moins connues du Portugal, encore hors des sentiers battus. Elle fait partie des régions les plus diversifiées du pays, alliant montagnes et vallées verdoyantes, villages paisibles et longs rivages de sable. ◆ À lire : « Histoire du siège de Lisbonne » de José Saramago.

ACCÈS *À 20 km au nord de Coïmbra, à 2 h au nord de Lisbonne et 1 h au sud de Porto* · **PRIX** *€–€€* · **CHAMBRES** *100 chambres* · **RESTAURATION** *Spécialités locales et cuisine internationale* · **HISTOIRE** *Construit au début des années 1920, l'hôtel a ouvert en 1926. La rénovation intégrale, achevée en 2008, souligne le caractère historique de l'endroit, complété par un boutique-spa* · **LES « PLUS »** *Ambiance Belle Époque*

SANTA CLARA
1728

LISBON, PORTUGAL

SANTA CLARA
1728

Campo de Santa Clara 128, 1100-473 Lisbon, Portugal
Tel. + 351 964 362 816 · booking@silentliving.pt
www.silentliving.pt/houses/santa-clara-1728/

HOME FOR A WHILE

The national pantheon that is the last resting place of Portugal's great sons and daughters is one of the best-known and most striking monuments in Lisbon – and among those with the longest construction period. The completion of the memorial, which was originally intended to be a church dedicated to Saint Engrácia, took almost 300 years. As a result of this, it gave rise to a special idiom: when locals speak, tongue in cheek or rolling their eyes to heaven, of "obras (works) de Santa Engrácia", they are referring to a lengthy matter that never seems to come to an end. Fortunately the wonderful guest house named Santa Clara 1728, only a few steps away from the pantheon, does not meet this description, and was built in a much shorter time. The TAP pilot and hotelier João Rodrigues, in collaboration with the architect Manuel Aires Mateus, transformed this 18th-century mansion into one of the most pleasant places to stay in Lisbon today. Inside the historic house, harmonious shades of white and gray, local materials such as lime-stone marble from Sintra and pine wood, and designer items by Antonio Citterio, Carl Hansen and Davide Groppi create a modern,

minimalistic ambience with clean lines and lots of style. João Rodrigues, who lives on the top floor with his family, welcomes his guests as if they were friends, not strangers. There is no hotel sign outside and no reception desk inside: guests who stay here are intended to feel it is their temporary home. This includes personal sightseeing tips from the host, conversations with like-minded people in the dining room, and moments of peace in the garden – a delightful oasis amidst the bustle of Lisbon. ◆ Book to pack: "The Land at the End of the World" by Antonio Lobo Antunes.

DIRECTIONS *Situated on the romantic Campo de Santa Clara in Alfama, one of the oldest Moorish quarters of Lisbon, 7.5 km/4.5 miles from the airport ·* **RATES** *€€€–€€€€ ·* **ROOMS** *6 suites ·* **FOOD** *Breakfast is served at a communal table. Guests get outstanding tips for where to eat lunch and dinner ·* **HISTORY** *The townhouse dating from 1728 opened in 2017 as a family hotel and guest house ·* **X-FACTOR** *The Feira da Ladra antiques and flea market is held right in front of the house every Tuesday and Saturday*

EIN ZUHAUSE AUF ZEIT

Das nationale Pantheon, in dem die großen Söhne und Töchter Portugals bestattet sind, zählt zu den berühmtesten und markantesten Denkmälern von Lissabon – und zu denen mit der längsten Bauzeit: Fast 300 Jahre lang dauerte die Vollendung dieses Monuments, das ursprünglich eine der heiligen Engrácia geweihte Kirche werden sollte. Damit prägte es sogar eine eigene Redewendung: Sprechen Einheimische mit einem Augenzwinkern oder -rollen von „obras (Arbeiten) de Santa Engrácia", meinen sie langwierige, scheinbar niemals endende Angelegenheiten. Glücklicherweise nicht in diese Kategorie fällt das wundervolle Gasthaus Santa Clara 1728, das nur ein paar Schritte vom Pantheon entfernt steht und in weitaus kürzerer Zeit entstanden ist. Der TAP-Pilot und Hotelier João Rodrigues verwandelte das Palais aus dem 18. Jahrhundert gemeinsam mit dem Architekten Manuel Aires Mateus in eine der angenehmsten Adressen des heutigen Lissabons. Im Inneren des historischen Hauses sorgen harmonische Weiß- und Grautöne, lokale Materialien wie Kalksteinmarmor aus Sintra und Pinienholz sowie Designerstücke von Antonio Citterio, Carl Hansen und Davide Groppi für ein modern-minimalistisches Ambiente mit klaren Linien und viel Stil. João Rodrigues, der mit seiner Familie die oberste Etage bewohnt, empfängt seine Gäste nicht wie Fremde, sondern wie Freunde. Es gibt kein Hotelschild draußen und keine Rezeption drinnen – wer hier Station macht, soll ein Zuhause auf Zeit vorfinden. Dazu gehören auch persönliche Sightseeing-Tipps des Hausherrn, Gespräche mit Gleichgesinnten im Esszimmer und Momente der Ruhe im Garten; inmitten des lebhaften Lissabons eine zauberhafte Oase. ◆ Buchtipp: „Ich gehe wie ein Haus in Flammen" von Antonio Lobo Antunes.

ANREISE *Am romantischen Campo de Santa Clara in Alfama gelegen, einem der ältesten maurischen Viertel Lissabons, 7,5 km vom Flughafen entfernt ·* PREIS *€€€–€€€€ ·* ZIMMER *6 Suiten ·* KÜCHE *Frühstück wird an der Gemeinschaftstafel serviert. Für Mittag- und Abendessen bekommt man ausgezeichnete Restauranttipps ·* GESCHICHTE *Der Stadtpalast anno 1728 wurde 2017 als Familien- und Gästehaus eröffnet ·* X-FAKTOR *Direkt vor der Tür findet jeden Dienstag und Samstag der Antiquitäten- und Flohmarkt Feira da Ladra statt*

UN CHEZ-SOI TEMPORAIRE

Le Panthéon national, dans lequel sont inhumés celles et ceux qui ont marqué l'histoire du Portugal, est l'un des monuments les plus célèbres et les plus remarquables de Lisbonne – et l'un de ceux dont la construction a duré le plus longtemps : il a fallu presque trois siècles pour terminer ce bâtiment, qui devait initialement devenir une église consacrée à Saint Engrácia. On lui doit même un adage : quand les habitants parlent avec un clin d'œil ou en roulant des yeux des « obras (œuvres) de Santa Engrácia », ils pensent à des affaires qui semblent ne jamais finir. Heureusement, la magnifique auberge Santa Clara 1728, à quelques pas du Panthéon, a été construite beaucoup plus rapidement et n'entre pas dans cette catégorie. En collaboration avec l'architecte Manuel Aires Mateus, le pilote chez TAP et hôtelier João Rodrigues a transformé l'hôtel particulier du XVIIIe siècle en l'une des adresses les plus agréables de Lisbonne aujourd'hui. À l'intérieur de la maison historique, des nuances harmonieuses de blanc et de gris, des matériaux locaux comme le marbre de Sintra et le bois de pin ainsi que des pièces design signées Antonio Citterio, Carl Hansen et Davide Groppi génèrent une ambiance moderne minimaliste aux lignes claires et élégantes. João Rodrigues, qui vit au dernier étage avec sa famille, accueille ses hôtes comme il accueillerait des amis. Il n'y a pas d'enseigne à l'extérieur et pas de réception à l'intérieur – si vous vous arrêtez ici, vous y serez chez vous pour un temps, bénéficiant des conseils touristiques de l'hôte, des conversations avec des semblables dans la salle à manger et savourant le calme du jardin ; une oasis magique au cœur de Lisbonne si animée. ◆ À lire : « Le Retour des caravelles » d'Antonio Lobo Antune.

ACCÈS *Près du Campo de Santa Clara à Alfama, l'un des plus anciens quartiers maures de Lisbonne. À 7,5 km de l'aéroport ·* PRIX *€€€–€€€€ ·* CHAMBRES *6 suites ·* RESTAURATION *Le petit déjeuner est servi à la table commune. De très bons conseils pour trouver un très bon restaurant midi et soir ·* HISTOIRE *L'hôtel particulier datant de 1728 a ouvert ses portes en 2017 comme maison d'hôtes et maison familiale ·* LES « PLUS » *Tous les mardi et samedi, le marché aux puces Feira da Ladra a lieu au pied de la porte*

SÃO LOURENÇO DO BARROCAL

MONSARAZ, ALENTEJO, PORTUGAL

SÃO LOURENÇO DO BARROCAL

7200-177 Monsaraz, Portugal
Tel: + 351 266 247 140 · reservations@barrocal.pt
www.barrocal.pt

FAMILY TRADITION

For 150 years this farmland in the Alentejo belonged to the family of José António Uva, until the Portuguese government nationalised it after the revolution of 1974. When the Uvas regained the estate some time later, it was abandoned and decayed. It seemed almost impossible to bring it back to life, but with a team of arch-aeologists, historians, landscape gardeners, architects and interior designers, José António Uva succeeded in creating a unique all-round work of art. The Pritzker Prize-winner Eduardo Souto de Moura found a balance between old architectural structures and modern use: he converted the former workers' quarters of the "monte" (peasant village) to rooms for guests, accommodated the restaurant in what had been the dog kennels and installed the bar in a disused space for an olive press. Wherever possible he recycled original materials such as terracotta, granite or wood, and where something new was needed, he had it made according to traditional methods. Working with local products, the Anahory Almeida studio from Lisbon, which belongs to Uva's wife Ana,

carried out the interior design with a combination of modern minimalistic lines and Portuguese craftwork. São Lourenço do Barrocal is not only a country hotel but also a working farm that produces grapes and olives, fruit and vegetables. Cows, horses and more than 75 species of birds populate the estate – and you need time to explore its 780 hectares, as a walk across the whole site takes a good six hours. ◆ Book to pack: "Raised from the Ground" by José Saramago.

DIRECTIONS *Situated below the medieval village of Monsaraz, 165 km/ 102 miles east of Lisbon airport ·* **RATES** *€€€–€€€€ ·* **ROOMS** *22 rooms, 2 suites, 16 cottages with 1, 2 or 3 bedrooms ·* **FOOD** *Fresh, rustic Alentejo dishes with a modern twist. The open-air grill restaurant has lots of atmosphere ·* **HISTORY** *7,000-year-old menhirs on the site speak of a long history. The hotel was opened in 2016 ·* **X-FACTOR** *The Susanne Kaufmann Spa with organic wellness products*

FAMILIENTRADITION

150 Jahre gehörte dieses Bauernland im Alentejo der Familie von José António Uva, ehe Portugals Regierung es nach der Revolution 1974 verstaatlichte. Als die Uvas es einige Zeit später zurück bekamen, war es verlassen und verfallen. Ein Wiederbeleben schien fast unmöglich, doch mit einem Team von Archäologen, Historikern, Landschaftsgärtnern, Architekten und Innenausstattern gelang José António Uva ein einzigartiges Gesamtkunstwerk. Pritzker-Preisträger Eduardo Souto de Moura fand die Balance zwischen alten architektonischen Strukturen und modernem Nutzen: Aus den ehemaligen Arbeiterunterkünften des „monte" (Bauerndorf) machte er Gästezimmer, brachte das Restaurant im einstigen Hundezwinger unter und die Bar in der stillgelegten Olivenpresse. Wo immer möglich, recycelte er Originalmaterialien wie Terrakotta, Granit oder Holz, und wo Neues vonnöten war, ließ er es nach überlieferten Techniken herstellen. Mit einheimischen Produkten arbeitete auch das Lissabonner Studio Anahory Almeida, welches Uvas Frau Ana gehört und das Interior Design entwarf, eine Kombination aus modern-minimalistischen Linien und portugiesischem Kunsthandwerk. São Lourenço do Barrocal ist nicht nur ein Landhotel, sondern auch ein Landwirtschaftsbetrieb, der Weintrauben und Oliven, Obst und Gemüse kultiviert. Auf dem Gelände leben Kühe, Pferde und mehr als 75 Vogelarten – wer die 780 Hektar erkunden möchte, braucht Zeit: Die Wanderung über das gesamte Grundstück dauert gute sechs Stunden. ◆ Buchtipp: „Hoffnung im Alentejo" von José Saramago.

ANREISE *Unterhalb des mittelalterlichen Dorfs Monsaraz, 165 km östlich des Flughafens Lissabon ·* PREIS *€€€–€€€€ ·* ZIMMER *22 Zimmer, 2 Suiten, 16 Cottages mit einem, 2 oder 3 Schlafzimmern ·* KÜCHE *Frische, rustikale Alentejo-Gerichte mit modernem Touch. Stimmungsvoll ist das Grillrestaurant unter freiem Himmel ·* GESCHICHTE *7000 Jahre alte Menhire auf dem Gelände zeugen von seiner langen Historie. Das Hotel wurde 2016 eröffnet ·* X-FAKTOR *Das Susanne-Kaufmann-Spa mit organischer Wellnesslinie*

TRADITION FAMILIALE

Ce domaine agricole de l'Alentejo a appartenu à la famille de José António Uva pendant 150 ans avant d'être nationalisé par le gouvernement portugais suite à la révolution de 1974 – quand les Uva l'ont récupéré quelque temps après, il était à l'abandon et délabré. Le faire revivre semblait presque impossible, mais avec une équipe d'archéologues, d'historiens, de paysagistes, d'architectes et de décorateurs, José António Uva a créé une œuvre d'art unique. Le lauréat du prix Pritzker, Eduardo Souto de Moura, a trouvé l'équilibre entre les anciennes structures architecturales et l'usage moderne : il a transformé les anciens quartiers ouvriers du « monte » en chambres d'hôtes, installé le restaurant dans l'ancien chenil et le bar dans le pressoir à olives désaffecté. Dans la mesure du possible, il a recyclé les matériaux d'origine tels que la terre cuite, le granit ou le bois, et là où quelque chose de nouveau était nécessaire, il l'a fait fabriquer selon des techniques traditionnelles. Le studio Anahory Almeida de Lisbonne, propriété de l'épouse d'Uva, Ana, et responsable de la décoration intérieure, a également travaillé avec des produits locaux, alliant des lignes minimalistes modernes à l'artisanat portugais. São Lourenço do Barrocal n'est pas seulement un hôtel de campagne, c'est aussi une exploitation agricole qui cultive de la vigne et des olives, des fruits et des légumes. Vaches, chevaux et plus de 75 espèces d'oiseaux vivent sur le domaine – si vous voulez explorer les 780 hectares, vous avez besoin de temps : la promenade à travers toute la propriété dure six heures. ◆ À lire : « Relevé de terre » de José Saramago.

ACCÈS *En-dessous du village médiéval de Monsaraz, à 165 km à l'est de l'aéroport de Lisbonne ·* PRIX *€€€–€€€€ ·* CHAMBRES *22 chambres, 2 suites, 16 cottages abritant 1, 2 ou 3 chambres à coucher ·* RESTAURATION *Des plats de l'Alentejo frais et rustiques avec une touche moderne. Le restaurant-barbecue en plein air a une ambiance particulière ·* HISTOIRE *Des menhirs de 7 000 ans sur la propriété témoignent de sa longue histoire. L'hôtel a été ouvert en 2016 ·* LES « PLUS » *Le spa Susanne Kaufmann avec sa ligne bien-être bio*

SUBLIME COMPORTA

GRÂNDOLA, SETÚBAL, PORTUGAL

SUBLIME COMPORTA

EN 261-1 Muda, CCI 3954 Grândola 7570-337, Portugal
Tel: + 351 269 449 376 · info@sublimecomporta.pt
www.sublimecomporta.pt
Open from early March to late January

CHIC IN COMPORTA

For a long time Comporta was mainly known for its fishing port, salt production and rice cultivation – and for its famous owner, the Portuguese Espírito Santo Bank, which went bankrupt a few years ago, however. Now this town on the Atlantic coast has also become a discreet retreat for rich and influential people: the Grimaldis and Sarkozys take holidays here, and with a bit of luck you can bump into Philippe Starck or Christian Louboutin. When Patricia and Gonçalo Pessoa, then a flight attendant and pilot for the airline TAP, discovered Comporta in 2004, they fell in love with its relaxed blend of nature and bohemian atmosphere straightaway, bought some land and started to build. What was originally intended as a private holiday home has evolved in the meantime to the Sublime Comporta. Its modern architecture and minimalistic interior are reminiscent of the traditional rice storing facilities and cabanas of Comporta (and slightly resemble the Aman Hotels). Rustic wood, straw, leather and linen are combined with designer items, and the interior and exterior worlds are linked together almost seamlessly. The owners attach as much importance to sustainability as to style: the house operates its own water treatment system, heats the floors and pool with solar energy, and has an organic restaurant in the middle of the garden. ◆ Book to pack: "Night Train to Lisbon" by Pascal Mercier.

DIRECTIONS *Situated on a 17-hectare estate with pines and cork oaks (8 km/5 miles from the nearest beach), 128 km/80 miles south of Lisbon airport* · **RATES** *€€ (room), €€€ (suite), €€€€ (villa), minimum stay 2–4 nights during the high season* · **ROOMS** *23 rooms and suites, and 22 villas with 2–5 bedrooms and private pool* · **FOOD** *Sem Porta serves seasonal Portuguese dishes. The Food Circle serves organic meals for a maximum of 12 guests* · **HISTORY** *Opened in 2014* · **X-FACTOR** *The spa with products by Amala Organic Skincare*

DER CHIC COMPORTAS

Lange Zeit war Comporta vor allem für seine Fischerei, die Salzgewinnung und den Reisanbau bekannt – und für seinen berühmten Besitzer, die portugiesische Bank Espírito Santo, die vor einigen Jahren jedoch in Konkurs ging. Inzwischen ist der Ort an der Atlantikküste aber auch ein diskretes Refugium der Reichen und Einflussreichen: Die Grimaldis und Sarkozys urlauben hier, und mit etwas Glück kann man Philippe Starck oder Christian Louboutin über den Weg laufen. Als Patricia und Gonçalo Pessoa, damals Stewardess bzw. Pilot der TAP, Comporta 2004 entdeckten, verliebten sie sich auf der Stelle in die entspannte Mischung aus Natur und Boheme, kauften ein Grundstück und fingen an zu bauen. Was ursprünglich als privates Feriendomizil gedacht war, hat sich inzwischen zum Sublime Comporta entwickelt. Die moderne Architektur und das minimalistische Interieur erinnern an die traditionellen Reisspeicher und Cabanas von Comporta (und ein bisschen an die Aman-Hotels); rustikales Holz, Stroh, Leder und Leinen werden mit Designerstücken kombiniert und Innen- und Außenwelten beinahe schwellenlos miteinander verbunden. Auf Nachhaltigkeit legen die Besitzer ebenso viel Wert wie auf Stil. So besitzt das Haus ein eigenes Wasseraufbereitungssystem, heizt Böden und Pool mit Solarenergie und bietet ein organisches Erlebnisrestaurant mitten im Biogarten. ◆ Buchtipp: „Nachtzug nach Lissabon" von Pascal Mercier.

ANREISE *Auf einem 17-Hektar-Anwesen mit Pinien und Korkeichen gelegen (8 km zum nächsten Strand), 128 km südlich des Flughafens Lissabon ·* **PREIS** *€€ (Zimmer), €€€ (Suite), €€€€ (Villa), 2–4 Nächte Mindestaufenthalt während der Hochsaison ·* **ZIMMER** *23 Zimmer und Suiten sowie 22 Villen mit 2–5 Schlafzimmern und Privatpool ·* **KÜCHE** *Das „Sem Porta" kocht portugiesisch. Maximal 12 Gäste finden im organischen „Food Circle" Platz ·* **GESCHICHTE** *2014 eröffnet ·* **X-FAKTOR** *Das Spa mit Produkten von Amala Organic Skincare*

LE CHIC DE COMPORTA

Pendant longtemps, Comporta a surtout été connue pour sa pêche, ses salines et ses rizières – et pour son célèbre propriétaire, la famille portugaise Espírito Santo, dont la banque a fait faillite il y a quelques années. Aujourd'hui, ce village situé sur la côte atlantique est devenu un refuge discret pour les riches et les influents : les Grimaldi et les Sarkozy y passent leurs vacances, et avec un peu de chance vous pourrez croiser Philippe Starck ou Christian Louboutin. Lorsque Patricia et Gonçalo Pessoa, alors stewardess et pilote de TAP Air Portugal, ont découvert Comporta en 2004 lors d'une escale, ils sont immédiatement tombés amoureux de cet endroit qui marie de manière décontractée la nature et l'esprit bohème, ont acheté un terrain et commencé à construire. Ce qui devait être à l'origine une maison de vacances à usage privé s'est transformé en Sublime Comporta. L'architecture moderne et l'intérieur minimaliste évoquent les entrepôts de riz et les cabanes traditionnelles de Comporta (et un peu les hôtels Aman) ; le bois rustique, la paille, le cuir et le lin sont combinés avec des pièces design, et l'intérieur et l'extérieur sont parfaitement connectés. Les propriétaires attachent autant d'importance à la durabilité qu'au style. La maison possède son propre système de traitement des eaux, chauffe les sols et la piscine à l'aide de l'énergie solaire, et dans le jardin bio, un restaurant bio offre des expériences gastronomiques uniques. ◆ À lire : « Train de nuit pour Lisbonne » de Pascal Mercier.

ACCÈS *Sur un domaine de 17 hectares où poussent des pins et des chênes liège (à 8 km de la plage la plus proche), à 128 km au sud de l'aéroport de Lisbonne ·* **PRIX** *€€ (chambre), €€€ (suite), €€€€ (villa). Séjour minimum de 2–4 nuits pendant la haute saison ·* **CHAMBRES** *23 chambres et suites ainsi que 22 villas abritant 2–5 chambres à coucher, piscine privée ·* **RESTAURATION** *Le « Sem Porta » propose une cuisine portugaise de saison. Le « Food Circle » peut accueillir 12 clients maximum ·* **HISTOIRE** *Ouvert en 2014 ·* **LES « PLUS »** *Le spa qui propose des produits d'Amala Organic Skincare*

REID'S PALACE

FUNCHAL, MADEIRA, PORTUGAL

REID'S PALACE

Estrada Monumental 139, 9000-098 Funchal, Madeira, Portugal
Tel. + 351 291 71 71 71 · reservations.rds@belmond.com
www.belmond.com/reidspalace

GRACE AND FAVOR

For generations this grand old hotel has been the epitome of grace. Reid's Palace has served as a home away from home to many of the most well-known people of the last century. The guest book is a roll call of celebrities. Anybody who was, or is still, somebody has stayed here at one time. So little seems to have changed that one might picture Winston Churchill taking afternoon tea on the terrace; Elisabeth, the Empress of Austria, gazing out to sea from her veranda; or imagine watching George Bernard Shaw being taught the tango on the lawn. The old-fashioned charm continues to draw the rich and famous, as well as the not yet renowned. Part of the attraction is the setting on the island of Madeira. High up on the clifftops overlooking the Bay of Funchal and the Atlantic, the hotel's site adds to the privacy of its guests. Staying here is almost like being on the "grand tour"; but the days of luxury travel are not recreated here: in fact, it has always been like this. Reid's Palace evokes eras that were more gracious and less hurried than the one we live in now. Time has been kind to this lovely old landmark. ◆ Book to pack: "Pygmalion" by George Bernard Shaw.

DIRECTIONS *22 km/14 miles from Madeira international airport ·* RATES *€€€ ·* ROOMS *130 rooms and 34 suites ·* FOOD *5 restaurants to choose from ·* HISTORY *The original hotel was built and opened in 1891. In 1967 an extension was built ·* X-FACTOR *The hotel is an historical legend*

RUHM UND EHRE

Seit Generationen war dieses große alte Hotel der Inbegriff von Eleganz. Im Reid's Palace fanden viele bekannte Persönlichkeiten des letzten Jahrhunderts eine zweite Heimat. Alle Berühmtheiten haben – so scheint es – schon einmal hier gewohnt. Und so wenig haben sich die Zeiten offenbar geändert, dass man sich noch immer Winston Churchill beim Nachmittagstee auf der Terrasse vorstellen kann oder die österreichische Kaiserin Elisabeth, berühmt als Sisi, wie sie von ihrer Veranda aus auf das Meer blickt, oder George Bernard Shaw, der auf dem Rasen Tango lernt. Ungebrochen scheint der altmodische Charme des Hotels wie ein Magnet auf die Reichen und Schönen zu wirken, aber ebenso auf die nicht wirklich oder noch nicht Berühmten. Ein weiterer Anziehungspunkt ist die Lage des Hotels. Hoch über den Klippen errichtet, bietet es einen Blick über die Bucht von Funchal auf den Atlantik und schützt durch seine exponierte Lage die Privatsphäre der Gäste. Wer hier zu Gast ist, wird sich fühlen wie damals die junge Boheme, die durch die Welt reiste, um ihren Horizont zu erweitern. Aber hier muss die Vergangenheit nicht künstlich wiedererweckt werden, hier ist es einfach so, wie es schon immer gewesen ist. An diesem Ort, zu dem die Zeit so freundlich war, darf man noch einmal am Charme und an der Ruhe früherer Zeiten teilhaben. ◆ Buchtipps: „Pygmalion" von George Bernard Shaw und „Churchill" von Sebastian Haffner.

ANREISE *22 km vom Flughafen Madeira International gelegen* · PREIS *€€€* · ZIMMER *130 Zimmer und 34 Suiten* · KÜCHE *5 Restaurants stehen zur Auswahl* · GESCHICHTE *Das ursprüngliche Hotel wurde 1891 gebaut und eröffnet; 1967 kam ein Anbau hinzu* · X-FAKTOR *Das Hotel ist ein historisches Schwergewicht*

RETRAITE DES CÉLÉBRITÉS

Symbole d'élégance depuis des générations, le Reid's Palace a accueilli maintes célébrités du siècle passé, comme en témoigne son livre d'or. Tous les grands personnages ont séjourné au moins une fois en ces lieux. Le cadre a si peu changé que l'on imagine sans peine Winston Churchill prendre le thé sur la terrasse, Sissi, impératrice d'Autriche, scruter la mer depuis sa véranda, ou George Bernard Shaw prendre des cours de tango sur la pelouse. Le charme désuet continue d'attirer les grands et les moins grands de ce monde. L'un des atouts de l'hôtel est sa situation sur l'île de Madère. Perché sur les falaises dominant la baie de Funchal et l'Atlantique, il offre la retraite discrète recherchée par la clientèle. Un séjour dans ce palace évoque les somptueux voyages de la haute société d'autrefois ; mais le luxe n'a pas été recréé. Ici, il existe depuis toujours. Le Reid's Palace rappelle une époque plus raffinée et moins agitée que celle d'aujourd'hui. Le temps a su épargner cet endroit plein de charme et de chic. ◆ À lire : « Pygmalion » de George Bernard Shaw.

ACCÈS *À 22 km de l'aéroport Madeira International* · PRIX *€€€* · CHAMBRES *130 chambres et 34 suites* · RESTAURATION *5 restaurants au choix* · HISTOIRE *L'hôtel a été construit et a ouvert en 1891. Une annexe a été ajoutée en 1967* · LES « PLUS » *Un hôtel parmi les plus riches du point de vue historique*

PHOTO CREDITS

IMPRINT

EACH AND EVERY TASCHEN BOOK PLANTS A SEED!
TASCHEN is a carbon-neutral publisher. Each year, we offset our annual carbon emissions with carbon credits at the Instituto Terra, a reforestation program in Minas Gerais, Brazil, founded by Lélia and Sebastião Salgado. To find out more about this eco-logical partnership, please check: www.taschen.com/zerocarbon
Inspiration: unlimited. Carbon footprint: zero.

To stay informed about TASCHEN and our upcoming titles, please subscribe to our free magazine at www.taschen.com/magazine, follow us on Twitter, Instagram, and Facebook, or e-mail your questions to contact@taschen.com.

© 2020 TASCHEN GmbH
Hohenzollernring 53, D-50672 Köln
www.taschen.com

Printed in Slovenia
ISBN 978–3–8365–7807–3

EDITING, ART DIRECTION AND LAYOUT
Angelika Taschen, Berlin

PROJECT MANAGER
Stephanie Paas, Cologne

DESIGN
Maximiliane Hüls, Cologne

PRODUCTION
Ute Wachendorf, Cologne

GERMAN TRANSLATION
Claudia Egdorf, Düsseldorf
Gabriele-Sabine Gugetzer, Hamburg

ENGLISH TRANSLATION
John Sykes, Cologne

FRENCH TRANSLATION
Delphine Nègre-Bouvet, Paris
Michèle Schreyer, Cologne

THE EDITOR
Angelika Taschen studied art history and German literature in Heidelberg, gaining her doctorate in 1986. Working for TASCHEN from 1987, she has published numerous titles on art, architecture, photography, design, travel, and lifestyle.

THE AUTHORS
Christiane Reiter is a freelance author based in Brussels. She studied journalism at the University of Eichstätt and worked as a travel editor for Ringier Publishing in Munich and Zurich. Later, she established the travel section of the *Frankfurter Allgemeine Sonntagszeitung*.

Shelley-Maree Cassidy is a writer and marketing specialist who has written two books on hotels around the world and has contributed travel articles to magazines and journals. Her particular interest in hotels stems from her family background - as her great-grandparents owned several of the first hotels in New Zealand, where she lives.

FRONT COVER
Tannerhof, Bayrischzell, Bavaria.
Photo: Supplied by the hotel

BACK COVER
Casa Iris, Orbetello. Photo: Serena Eller/Vega MG

ENDPAPERS
Mezi Plůtky, Čeladná. Photo: Romana Bennet;
Supplied by the hotel

PRICE CATEGORIES
€ up to 150 € · €€ up to 250 € ·
€€€ up to 450 € · €€€€ over 450 €